THE STORM IS COMING

PERSECUTION FOR CHRIST'S SAKE

D1557140

THE STORM IS COMING

PERSECUTION FOR CHRIST'S SAKE

by
Frank R. Shivers

LIGHTNING SOURCE
1246 Heil Quaker Blvd.
La Vergne, TN

Copyright 2021 by
Frank Shivers Evangelistic Association
All rights reserved
Printed in the United States of America

Unless otherwise noted, Scripture quotations are from
The Holy Bible *King James Version*

Library of Congress Cataloging-in-Publication Data

Shivers, Frank R., 1949-
Persecution for Christ's Sake / Frank Shivers
ISBN 978-1-878127-45-7

Library of Congress Control Number:
2021909664

Cover design by
Tim King

For Information:
Frank Shivers Evangelistic Association
P. O. Box 9991
Columbia, South Carolina 29290
www.frankshivers.com

Presented to

_____

by

_____

Date

_____

Laughter, ridicule, opposition and persecution are often
the only reward which Christ's followers get from the world.[1]
~ J. C. Ryle

"For unto you it is given in the behalf of Christ, not only to believe
on him, but also to suffer for his sake."
~ Philippians 1:29

To

Them "of whom the world is not worthy"—
the persecuted Christian.
It is with overwhelming gratitude for their
stand, service, sacrifice, and suffering "for Christ's
sake" that this volume is dedicated.

and

Johnny and Loraine Mellette
In profound appreciation for their kindness,
graciousness and support.

"Christians are persecuted for the sake of righteousness because of their loyalty to Christ. Real loyalty to Him creates friction in the hearts of those who pay Him only lip service. Loyalty arouses their consciences and leaves them with only two alternatives: follow Christ or silence Him. Often their only way of silencing Christ is by silencing His servants. Persecution, in subtle or less subtle forms, is the result."[2]

~ Sinclair Ferguson

Am I a soldier of the Cross—
    A follower of the Lamb?
And shall I fear to own His cause
    Or blush to speak His name?

Must I be carried to the skies
    On flowery beds of ease,
While others fought to win the prize
    And sailed through bloody seas?

Are there no foes for me to face?
    Must I not stem the flood?
Is this vile world a friend to grace
    To help me on to God?

Sure, I must fight if I would reign;
    Increase my courage, Lord!
I'll bear the toil, endure the pain,
    Supported by Thy Word.

Thy saints in all this glorious war
    Shall conquer though they die;
They see the triumph from afar
    By faith's discerning eye.

When that illustrious day shall rise
    And all thy armies shine
In robes of victory through the skies,
    The glory shall be thine.

~ Isaac Watts (1724)

Contents

Introduction

The Christian is forewarned about the likelihood of persecution and told to expect it from various quarters. It may arise from governments, religious systems, the world at large or even the family—siblings, parents and children betraying one another (Matthew 10:17, 21).

To speak out biblical specificities in regard to morality, ethics, convictions, and doctrinal beliefs "for Christ's sake" brings bitter and venomous opposition and oppression (censorship of speech, defamation of character, discrimination, intolerance, ostracization, confiscation of property, revocation of sponsorship, religious liberty restraint, boycott, slanderous accusation, bombing and burning of churches, torture, execution, etc.). It's unavoidable. "When you openly live a godly life," states John MacArthur, "you will bang heads with Satan. You will confront the world, and persecution will be automatic."[3] Thomas Watson said, "The saints have no charter of exemption from trials. Though they live ever so meek, merciful, pure in heart, their piety will not shield them from sufferings. The way to Heaven is by way of thorns and blood. Though it be full of roses in regard of the comforts of the Holy Spirit, yet it is full of thorns in regard of persecutions."[4] It is in such persecutions the Christian reveals his true identity and colors.

A misconception of persecution which leads to unawareness of its presence in our time and place is the thought that it's always to be physically torturous. It is believed that since Christians in America, for example, are not being beaten with whips, dragged out of town by their heels or executed for the faith, persecution is nonexistent here. But such thinking cannot be further from the truth. Jesus taught that persecution is persecution, regardless of its *form* of antagonism (Matthew 5:11). And every faithful Christian experiences it (2 Timothy 3:12). The present "mild" persecution evidenced in the West (compared to that of the first-century church) is a foreshadowing of a greater to come. Franklin Graham said concerning anti-Christian persecution, "The storm is coming."[5]

Already the formation of thick dark clouds of persecution for the church may be seen on the horizon.

Persecution may not be encountered each day of the Christian life, but it will be experienced all the days of the Christian life. J. G. Morrison tells a story (undocumented) about John Wesley which illustrates the point. He writes, "John Wesley was riding along on his horse one day when it dawned on him that three days had passed in which he had suffered no persecution. Not a brick or an egg had been thrown for three days. Alarmed, he stopped his horse and exclaimed, 'Could it be that I have sinned and am backslidden?' Slipping from his horse, Wesley went down on his knees and began interceding with God to show him where, if any, there was a fault.

"A rough fellow on the other side of the hedge, hearing the prayer, looked across and recognized the preacher. 'I'll fix that Methodist preacher,' he said, picking up a brick and tossing it over at him.

"It missed its mark and fell harmlessly beside John, whereupon Wesley leaped to his feet joyfully exclaiming, 'Thank you, Lord! I know I still have Your presence.'"[6] He that walks devotedly with Christ will encounter persecution at various points and times. And if not, he ought to be concerned as to why he isn't.

Time spent in adversity "for Christ's sake" (not obnoxious or selfish reasons) is not to be counted loss, but gain (personal edification, furtherance of the Gospel, exaltation of Christ and the evangelization of sinners). Paul said that to suffer religious persecution was a privilege, honor or favor afforded the believer by Christ (Philippians 1:29) and was to be endured, therefore, with joy (Romans 5:3). See James 1:12. An unknown jailed Chinese pastor said, "Persecution is an honor we must deserve, and its reward is a clearer vision of the face of Christ."[7] It is said that the apostles "departed from the presence of the council [Sanhedrin] rejoicing that they were counted worthy to suffer shame for his name" (Acts 5:41). Guy de Brez, imprisoned in Belgium for Christ's sake, was asked by a visitor how he could eat or drink or sleep in quiet. "Madam," said he, "my chains neither terrify me nor break my sleep; on the contrary, I glory and take delight therein, esteeming them at a higher rate than chains and rings of gold or jewels of any price whatever. The rattling of my chains is like the effect of an instrument of music in my ears—not that such an effect comes merely from my chains, but it is because I am bound therewith for maintaining the truth of the Gospel."[8]

Foundational tenets of persecution—its source (Satan and his emissaries), subject (Christ and His followers), strategy (infliction of pain and suffering to silence and dishearten believers), scope (variation in form and severity, at times barbaric and inhumane), sphere (spiritual, political, cultural and social realms), speed (swiftness in its expansion and intensification) and stymieing (its obstruction and defeat through the believers' strong faith, courage and dependence upon Christ)—are expatiated in this book to alert saints to its nature and eventuality (if not presently experienced) and to enhance preparedness to meet and endure it "as a good soldier of Jesus Christ" (2 Timothy 2:3). Additionally, inspiration and encouragement are presented for the persecuted (the persecuted church) from the pens of history's greatest saints and martyrs and the Holy Scriptures, as well as challenges for their undergirding and support (Chapter 28).

My prayer is that with the turn of each page the reader may be either enlightened about persecution, encouraged in persecution, and/or enabled to bear persecution "for Christ's sake." May we so live and suffer "for Christ's sake" that in Heaven Christ will say unto us, "Well done, good and faithful servant. You have been faithful over a little; I will set you over much. Enter into the joy of your master" (Matthew 25:23 ESV).

Jesus, our help in time of need,
　　Thy suffering servants see,
Who would in all Thy footsteps tread
　　And bear the cross with Thee.

Stand by us in this evil hour,
　　Our feeble souls defend,
And in our weakness show Thy power,
　　And keep us to the end.

The world and their infernal god
　　Against Thy people rise;
Because our trust is in Thy blood
　　They mingle earth and skies.

Slaughter and cruel threats they breathe
　　And endless battles wage
And gnash upon us with their teeth
　　And tear the ground with rage.

Captain of our salvation, hear.
　　In all the heathen's sight
Make bare Thine arm. Appear, appear
　　And for Thy people fight.

Jesus, Thy righteous cause maintain,
　　The sons of violence quell,
Take to Thee Thy great power, and reign
　　O'er Heaven and earth and Hell.

~ Charles Wesley (1744)

1
Theology of Biblical Persecution

"Blessed are ye, when men shall revile you, and persecute you, and shall say all manner of evil against you falsely, for my sake."[9]
~ Jesus

Persecution seeks to silence, banish, censor, control, or exterminate Christians and divorce them from their core biblical values and convictions, missionary enterprises, and allegiance to Jesus Christ. As unwelcome as persecution is, it is part and parcel of the Christian life (Matthew 5:11 and 2 Timothy 3:12). The instigator and strategist of all Christian persecution is Satan (1 Peter 5:8). "The biblical authors," states Christopher Byrley, "identify any opposition to the ministry of Jesus, including His sacrificial death, [and that of His followers] to be the work of Satan."[10]

The Greek word for *persecution,* used more than fifty times in the New Testament in some form, means "to prosecute, persecute, pursue with repeated acts of enmity [unfair or cruel treatment]."[11] It is a word used of wild beasts pursued by hunters or an enemy chased in flight.[12] Gardner says, "Persecution is a broad term, covering a wide range of hostile actions, while ridicule and slander both deal with verbal abuse."[13] Chuck Swindoll states, "It's [persecution] the idea of being chased, having others 'on our case,' we would say. It is an active, aggressive word conveying everything from being intimidated to being assaulted, actually attacked. Servants will suffer persecution."[14] Concisely, persecution may be defined as "any hostility experienced as a result of identification with Jesus Christ."[15] Persecution can inflict political (James 2:6; Nehemiah 6:1–9), religious (Acts 5:40), mental (Acts 5:28), social or discriminatory (2 Kings 24:14; Psalm 137:2–4, treated as outcasts), relational (Genesis 4:8), and/or physical harm (Exodus 22:23). And it is experienced by "all that will live godly in Christ Jesus" (2 Timothy 3:12). George Whitefield states, "To 'live godly in Christ,' is to make the divine will...the sole principle of all our thoughts, words, and actions."[16]

~ *Persecuted for Christ's Sake* ~

Persecution, though an honor, [it identifies the believer with Christ's suffering (1 Peter 4:13) and magnifies Christ unto the world (1 Peter 4:16)] is not to be pursued. It will unrelentingly pursue the believer. As D. A. Carson states, Christ (Matthew 5:11–12) "neither encourages seeking persecution nor permits retreating from it, sulking, or retaliation."[17]

It is not enough that the Christian only refrain from complicity with the world (this he must constantly guard against) and refuse to allow its antagonism to divert him from his worship and walk. He must as the good soldier of Christ endeavor to make Him known and see that biblical teaching is obeyed in the world.[18] He is to be a light that illuminates in the darkness of evil, and a block of salt that makes pure that which is wrong and preserves that which is good (Matthew 5:13–16). This is where the rubber meets the road, bringing opposition and persecution. Of this Jesus forewarned His disciples: "If the world hate you, ye know that it hated me before it hated you....The servant is not greater than his lord. If they have persecuted me, they will also persecute you" (John 15:18, 20). And Paul said, "For unto you it is given in the behalf of Christ, not only to believe on him, but also to suffer for his sake" (Philippians 1:29).

Spurgeon said, "Dream not that worldlings will admire you or that the more holy and the more Christlike you are, the more peaceably people will act towards you. They prized not the polished gem; how should they value the jewel in the rough?"[19] Billy Graham states, "I am afraid that we in the church are making a great mistake by trying to make Christianity popular and pleasant. We have taken away the cross and substituted cushions. But Christ said the world hated Him, and He predicted that it would hate us. He invited us not to a picnic but to a pilgrimage. He offered us not an excursion but an execution. Salvation is free, but discipleship costs everything we have."[20]

Persecution is a retaliatory action against Christ's person (righteous and redeemer), message (repentance and reconciliation), mission (redemption) and means (regeneration through His atoning blood) exacted upon all His followers. It will come, Jesus says, "because you trust in me" (Matthew 5:11 NLV) or "on account of me" and will be endless until His return. Following the 'narrow way' (Matthew 7:13–14) taught by Christ and building one's house upon the "Rock" (Matthew 7:24–25) precipitates persecution.[21] However, Jesus promises that when the rains, winds, and floods (in part symbolic of persecution) beat against the "house," it will not crumble or collapse (Matthew 7:24–25),[22] and that when the believer suffers persecution, He suffers it with them (Acts 9:4). What consolation to know the Shepherd so loves His sheep that He suffers with them in their maltreatment.

The believer that suffers and endures persecution (hostile opposition to the faith) for Christ's sake gains a reward (the crown of life, according to Revelation 2:10); is identified with biblical heroes of the faith ("so persecuted they the prophets"); has assurance of Heaven ("for theirs is the kingdom of heaven"); shares in the "fellowship of [Christ's] sufferings" (Philippians 3:10); develops spiritual maturity and endurance (James 1:2–4); serves as a pattern to the godly in suffering, enhanced usefulness, joy and power; and at times makes a significant difference for the cause of Christ.

There may be seasons of rest when the rage of persecution subsides, "yet, as long as there are any of 'the serpent's seed' on earth, 'the seed of the woman' will be treated by them as 'the filth of the world, and the offscouring of all things.'"[23] Therefore the Christian must have a mindset of continuous perseverance until the end. Endurance in persecution is enabled by the Holy Spirit (Acts 4:31), the household of faith (1 Thessalonians 3:6–8), Holy Scripture (Psalm 119:42), intimacy with Christ (Acts 4:13), example of the martyrs (Hebrews 11), faith (Psalm 27:12–13), faithful testimony to the truth (Revelation 12:11b), loving Christ supremely (Revelation 12:11c), and by the "blood of the Lamb" (Revelation 12:11a).

The endurance of the Christian church to survive centuries of oppression and opposition is best explained by a theology of persecution based upon belief in Jesus Christ as the Son of God who

Himself was persecuted and tormented and killed at Calvary, rose triumphantly from the dead Easter morning, ascended to Heaven forty days later, and is to return for the redeemed to take them to their new HOME. Man will endure the most horrendous torture and pain for what he is confident is true and real.

> Give us the wings of faith to rise
>   Within the veil and see
> The saints above—how great their joys,
>   How bright their glories be!
>
> Once they were mourning here below;
>   Their couch was wet with tears.
> They wrestled hard, as we do now,
>   With sins and doubts and fears.
>
> We ask them whence their victory came.
>   They, with united breath,
> Ascribe their conquest to the Lamb,
>   Their triumph to his death.
>
> They marked the footsteps that he trod,
>   His zeal inspired their breast,
> And, following their incarnate God,
>   Possess the promised rest.
>
> Our glorious Leader claims our praise
>   For His own pattern given,
> While the long cloud of witnesses
>   Show the same path to Heaven.

~ Isaac Watts (1709)

Witness and *martyr*. A distinction in the early church (and since) was made between believers who confessed Christ before authorities and survived with their lives, and those that did the same but were killed ("martyrs"), although both terms mean the same ("to witness or to testify"). Compare Acts 1:8 and Acts 22:20. Origen explained the reasoning for the distinction: "Now everyone who bears witness to the truth, whether he support it by words or deeds, or in whatever way, may properly be called a witness (martyr). But it has become the custom of the brotherhood, since they are struck with admiration of those who have contended to the death for truth and valor, to keep the name of *martyr* more properly for those who have borne witness to the mystery of godliness by shedding their blood for it."[24]

Upon the return of Christ, the curtain of persecution will fall (Revelation 22:12; 2 Thessalonians 2:8; 2 Timothy 4:8). The "victim" then will be the "victor." The "cross" then will be exchanged for the "crown." The righteous then will be vindicated (Revelation 6:10) and their tormentors eternally punished (Matthew 25:46; Revelation 21:8).

I shall not bear the cross thro' yon city,
    When the burdens of life are laid down.
When I knock on the portals of Heaven,
    I will trade the old cross for a crown.

Ev'ry cross that I bear for my Savior
    Will at last, when He calls, be laid down;
And my sorrows will all be forgotten,
    When I trade the old cross for a crown.

~ Johnson Oatman (1915)

Persecution is aggressive and widespread today. "From Sudan to Russia, from Nigeria to North Korea, from Colombia to India, followers of Christianity are targeted for their faith."[25] Christians are the most persecuted people in the world.[26] In the past 100 years more Christians have died in behalf of Christ than in all prior centuries since Jesus' time combined.[27] Annually 200 million Christians suffer some level of persecution.[28] The highest level of persecution of Christians the world has witnessed since the fall of the Soviet Union, occurred in 2014.[29] Every five minutes a Christian is martyred for his faith.[30] Persecution (though its form and intensity vary) is escalating numerically, geographically and in frequency.

This concise summary of the Biblical theology of persecution (aspects and facets) will be expounded upon in the rest of the book.

2
History of Biblical Persecution

"Let us not fear the opposition of men; every great movement in the Church from Paul down to modern times has been criticized on the ground that it promoted censoriousness [hypercriticism] *and intolerance and disputing. Of course the Gospel of Christ, in a world of sin and doubt, will cause disputing; and if it does not cause disputing and arouse bitter opposition, that is a fairly sure sign that it is not being faithfully proclaimed."*[31]

~ John Gresham Machen

The Old Testament is replete with cases of the believer's persecution by hostile entities. Abel was martyred by Cain (Matthew 23:35 and 1 John 3:12). David was persecuted by King Saul to protect his rule (1 Samuel 19:9–12) and by others for his personal faith (Psalm 7; Psalm 35; Psalm 119:84–87). Urijah was killed for prophesying that which displeased the king (Jeremiah 26:20–23). Tradition maintains that Amos experienced a violent death by the hands of Jeroboam II. Shadrach, Meshach, and Abednego were persecuted for unwillingness to bow to King Nebuchadnezzar's statue (Daniel 3:1). Daniel was persecuted for defying the king's order not to pray (Daniel 6:12–28). Jeremiah was persecuted (thrown into a cistern to die) for declaring what God told him to say (Jeremiah 38:1–6). Elijah was despised (1 Kings 18:17). The Psalms speak of the righteous suffering for the faith by the hand of the ungodly (Psalm 37 and Psalm 79). It is a plausible assumption, though not stated in the Bible, that Noah suffered harassment in the construction of the ark and for being a "preacher of righteousness" (2 Peter 2:5). Micaiah was hated (2 Chronicles 18:17). Zechariah was stoned to death for his prophetic condemnation under Joash (2 Chronicles 24:20–22). Nehemiah was oppressed and berated (Nehemiah 4). On a national level, the nation Israel suffered cruel persecution in Egypt (Exodus 1–3) and in exile (Psalm 137:1). Ancient Israel's history was one of continued suffering and affliction by ungodly oppressors (Judges 2:11–23).

In the New Testament, persecution began when King Herod sought to protect his dynasty by slaughtering every male two years old and under in the vicinity of Bethlehem in an attempt to kill the Christ Child who was to be born there (Matthew 2:16–18) and does not end until the final chapter of the book of Revelation. Spurgeon said, "Persecution set in as soon as the church appeared. The Man-Child was scarcely born into the world before the dragon began to pour forth floods out of his mouth, if perhaps he might utterly drown the woman's Seed. From that first day until now the page of history is crimson with the blood of the faithful. Surely the blood of saints, shed for the testimony of Jesus, might have filled the Mediterranean to its brim."[32]

The most notable cases of persecution cited in the New Testament, in addition to the aforementioned, include John the Baptist's imprisonment and beheading (Matthew 14:1–11), the chief priests' plot to arrest and murder Jesus (Luke 22:1–6), the continuous mocking and ridiculing of Jesus and the plot to have Him crucified (Matthew 27:29–31; Luke 23:36), Peter and John's arrest and flogging by the Sadducees (Acts 5:40), Stephen's arrest and stoning to death (Acts 7:54–60), the imprisonment of many believers by Saul (Paul) (Acts 8:3), King Herod's execution of James and imprisonment of Peter (Acts 12:1–5), Paul's stoning and being left for dead in Lystra (Acts 14:19), and Paul and Silas' flogging and imprisonment in Philippi (Acts 16:16–24).

Early church traditions indicate that all the apostles were martyred for Christ, except for John, who was exiled to the Isle of Patmos and died of old age. Peter and Andrew were crucified. James, the brother of John and the only apostle whose death is recorded in Scripture (Acts 12:2), was executed by King Herod. Phillip was said to have been stoned to death. Bartholomew (Nathaniel) was cast into the sea or crucified. Matthew was possibly stabbed to death or burned at the stake. Thomas was killed with a spear. James the son of Alphaeus was stoned to death. Simon the Zealot was sawed in half like Isaiah. Thaddeus was clubbed to death.[33] The form of the disciples' deaths may be uncertain or disputed, but not their faithfulness to Christ and mission amidst violent persecution and suffering until death occurred. People don't suffer or die for a lie. With the disciples there was no uncertainty regarding Christ's being the son of God and Savior of the world. Peter, speaking for all the disciples, said most emphatically, "We believe and are sure that thou art that Christ, the Son of the living God" (John 6:69). Persecution is endurable for what is known to be true.

Several Bible books like Hebrews, 1 Peter and Revelation were written to encourage persecuted believers (1 Peter 3:13–18; 4:12–19; 5:6–14; Hebrews 10:32–39; 12:3; Revelation 2–3)[34] while others were penned by Paul while suffering in prison (Ephesians, Philippians, Colossians, and Philemon). Acts details at least fifteen accounts of persecution. There are in the New Testament seventy-six general references to persecution and sixty-six specific references about Jesus' being persecution.[35]

3
Persecution Is Not an Anomaly

"Being misrepresented, slandered, reviled, persecuted, and wrong-fully accused is an inevitable part of being a Christian. We must expect to suffer unjustly. Our lives confront the culture we live in. We live as aliens in the world, and it should not surprise us when the world is hostile toward us (1 John 3:13). We were called for that purpose. In this world we will have tribulation (John 16:33). It goes with the territory."[36]

~ John MacArthur

It was prophesied by Christ that *all* His followers would be hated (Matthew 10:21) and persecuted (John 15:20) by the world. This has happened and is presently still happening. Billy Graham stated, "Persecution is one of the natural consequences of living the Christian life."[37] J. C. Ryle said, "Let it never surprise us, if we have to endure mockery, and ridicule, and false reports, because we belong to Christ. The disciple is not greater than His Master, nor the servant than His Lord."[38]

Persecution is not an anomaly or oddity but has been a com-monplace occurrence in Christianity since the first New Testament martyrs, John the Baptist's beheading and Stephen's stoning to death. W. S. Plumer wrote, "If we suffer reproach and persecution, nothing new has happened to us. Saul hunted David like a partridge upon the mountains. Shimei cursed David as if he had been the vilest of malefactors. Christ's murderers reviled him, and when dying taunted him."[39] Persecution was so commonplace for Paul that he said, "The Holy Spirit testifies to me in every city that imprisonment and *persecutions are waiting* for me" (Acts 20:23 NRSV). Nonethe-less, despite the danger, he took the message of the Cross into those very cities. A review of some of Paul's persecutions (certainly not all) is cited in Acts. He is kidnapped (Acts 21:27), beaten (Acts 21:30–31; 23:3), threatened (Acts 22:22; 27:42), arrested numerous times (Acts 21:33; 22:24; 23:35; 28:16), accused in lawsuits (Acts 22:30), interrogated (Acts 25:24–27), ridiculed (Acts 26:24), ignored (Acts 27:11), and shipwrecked (Acts 27:41). Paul said, "We both labor and suffer reproach, because we trust in the living God" (1 Timothy 4:10 NKJV).

Regarding persecution Peter wrote "Beloved, think it not strange concerning _the fiery trial_ which is to try you, _as though some strange thing happened_ unto you" (1 Peter 4:12). That is, when you suffer for righteousness' sake, don't think it is unusual or abnormal or something you shouldn't have expected ("strange"). View it as part and parcel of the normal Christian experience. Dietrich Bonhoeffer wrote, "To endure the Cross is not a tragedy; it is the suffering which is the fruit of an exclusive allegiance to Jesus Christ. When it comes, it is not an accident, but a necessity. It is not the sort of suffering which is inseparable from this mortal life, but the suffering which is an essential part of the specifically Christian life. It is not suffering per se, but suffering-and-rejection; and not rejection for any cause or conviction of our own, but rejection for the sake of Christ."[40]

The octopus' tentacles of persecution are being extended further and wider to impact more believers. Today seventy-five percent of Christians live in places where persecution is the norm.[41] On average, eight Christians died for their faith every day in 2019 (actual numbers vary drastically; this number is conservative). Additionally, 9,488 churches or Christian buildings were attacked and 3,711 Christians were detained without trial, arrested, sentenced and imprisoned.[42] Every month 722 forms of violence are committed against Christians.[43] Globally, persecution is not uncommon, not being persecuted is.

> Opposition is a normal mark of being a disciple of Jesus, as normal as hungering for righteousness or being merciful.
> D. A. Carson

Adrian Rogers says, "The new whipping boy in the world today is the Bible-believing Christian. He may be the most hated, persecuted person on earth. Bible Christians today endure everything from the limitations of their freedoms and civil rights to scorn and ridicule in the media. Many are going through prison, and many through death."[44] If privileged to suffer for the sake of Christ, count it all joy and take delight in it as Paul did (2 Corinthians 12:10). D. A. Carson states "It is no accident that Jesus should pass from peacemaking to persecution [Beatitudes], for the world enjoys its cherished hates and prejudices so much that the peacemaker is not always welcome. Opposition is a normal mark of being a disciple of Jesus, as normal as hungering for righteousness or being merciful."[45]

4
Principal Source of Persecution

"Satan is shown consistently to be the primary instigator of conflict against the ministry of Jesus and the Church. While this opposition usually involves the agency of human beings or institutions, within the biblical worldview, the ultimate source of this opposition was [is] the Devil himself."[46]

~ Christopher Byrley

The believer's enemy and the source and instigator behind all types and forms of persecution is Satan, the archenemy of God. The Bible says that "the whole world lies in the power of the evil one" (I John 5:19 CEV) and that Satan is the "ruler of this world" (John 12:31; 14:30; 16:11). This influence and power of Satan over the world's inhabitants is used to marshal their opposition to Christ, His followers and cause. (Sometimes he even deceives believers into opposing Christ, as happened to Peter in Matthew 16:23.) This is why Paul said, "For we are not fighting against people made of flesh and blood, but against persons without bodies—the evil rulers of the unseen world, those mighty satanic beings and great evil princes of darkness who rule this world; and against huge numbers of wicked spirits in the spirit world" (Ephesians 6:12 TLB). Saith Spurgeon, "The Christian soldier hath no gun and no sword, for he fighteth not with men. It is with 'spiritual wickedness in high places' that he fights, and with other principalities and powers than with those that sit on thrones and hold scepters in their hands."[47] This, says Barnes, is the source and origin of all spiritual conflicts, and with them the battle must be fought.[48] "Any individual, group, institution, or nation," writes Christopher Byrley, "that stands against God's people acts as an agent of Satan."[49]

All this explains the barbarism, viciousness and maliciousness of persecutors. John Calvin attests, "The state of the matter is this. Satan, the prince of the world, will never cease to fill his followers with rage, to carry on hostilities against the members of Christ. It is, no doubt, monstrous and unnatural that men who study to live a righteous life should be attacked and tormented in a way which they do not deserve."[50] Note, the followers of Satan in exacting persecution at his behest are "personally" responsible for the suffering they inflict and will be judged severely. Therefore Peter admonishes, "Be sober, be vigilant; because your adversary [enemy] the devil, as a roaring lion, walketh about [prowls], seeking whom he may devour [destroy]" (1 Peter 5:8). Despite persecution at the hands of the Devil's human agents, the Christian is assured of ultimate victory, for "greater is He that is in you, than he that is in the world" (1 John 4:4). See Chapter 6, *Criminality of Persecution.*

5
Causes for Persecution

"It is better to be divided by truth than to be united in error. It is better to speak the truth that hurts and then heals, than falsehood that comforts and then kills. It is better to be hated for telling the truth than to be loved for telling a lie. It is better to stand alone with the truth, than to be wrong with a multitude. It is better to ultimately succeed with the truth than to temporarily succeed with a lie. There is only one Gospel."[51]

~ Adrian Rogers

There are at minimum nine possible reasons as to why God allows Satan to persecute the saints.

(1. To ratify to the world the truth that the martyrs profess.[52]

(2. To enhance the faith in weaker and cowardly saints.[53] Paul's imprisonment served to instill confidence and courage in the Christians in Rome (Philippians 1:14).

(3. To enable the believer to identify with Christ in His sufferings.[54] See 1 Peter 4:13 and Philippians 3:10.

(4. To enlarge the kingdom of God on earth (John 12:24).

(5. To confirm the genuineness of the believer's faith (Matthew 13:21–22). See Chapter 10, *Persecution Authenticates Profession.*

(6. To purge the church of hypocrisy (Amos 9:9). Persecution brings sanctification. Spurgeon, in the sermon "The Sieve," remarked, "I know not whether every drop of the Atlantic Ocean might not have been incarminated [changed color] if the warm blood of all the martyrs had been poured into its all but boundless deeps. So many were the saints of God that were offered that arithmetic can scarcely compute their number. The church was sifted by these persecutions: the vain and light, the formal and the insincere went off from her, too glad to earn inglorious safety by dastardly apostasy. They could not afford to lose their lives for truth's sake; the cross was too heavy for their galled shoulder, and they turned

aside. Yet not the least true grain fell to the ground; the church was never the worse for her fiercest persecution. In fact, she seemed to derive new vigor from her baptism of blood, and her voice was never so piercing and so potent as when it was uplifted from the rack and the stake. Sifted she has been, but never injured; she has been a grand gainer through the grace of God by all her tribulations and afflictions. There must be these fiery persecutions, that the drossy hypocrites may be purged out."[55]

(7. To magnify the Lord. To magnify Christ is to exalt His person, elevate His position, elicit His praise, express His passion and emphasize His purity (righteousness and holiness). And it's in persecution the believer magnifies Christ the most. Billy Graham said, "We can take persecution because we know the purpose behind it. The purpose is to glorify [magnify] God."[56]

(8. To enhance evangelism and missions (Philippians 1:12–14). See Chapter 8, *Motivation for Suffering Persecution.*

(9. To enhance spiritual maturity (James 1:2–4).

What precipitates persecution of the saints (harassment, bullying, censorship, religious liberty restraint, hostility, torture, imprisonment, execution, etc.)? Persecution arises because of the clash of two irreconcilable value systems.[57] The clash is descriptively cited in 1 John: "Never give your hearts to this world or to any of the things in it. A man cannot love the Father and love the world at the same time. For the whole world-system, based as it is on men's primitive desires, their greedy ambitions and the glamour of all that they think splendid, is not derived from the Father at all, but from the world itself" (1 John 2:15–16 PHILLIPS). See John 15:19; Galatians 4:29, and Ephesians 5:11. Antagonism is inevitable between worldlings and Christians (John 15:18–19). Their values, convictions, and conduct differ (as revealed in the Sermon on the Mount, Matthew 5). And this antagonism brings persecution and oppression from the world. There are but two ways to end the antagonism outside of the return of Christ: either by lifting the world up to Christian principles and practice (Matthew 5:14–16) or bringing the same down to pacify the world.[58] May the former be passionately pursued, however difficult, and the latter bitterly opposed whatever the persecution.

Persecution arises from false and bogus accusation(s). The first persecution of Christians took place in A.D. 64 in Rome under Nero and was based on a whopping lie. Nero blamed the burning and dreadful conflagration of the city that he ordered (based on some historians) on the Christians. This he did to make room for the construction of his planned palatial complex, the Domus Aurea. John Foxe states, "This was the occasion of the first persecution, and the barbarities exercised on the Christians were such as even excited the commiseration of the Romans themselves. Nero even refined upon cruelty and contrived all manner of punishments for the Christians that the most infernal imagination could design. In particular, he had some sewed up in skins of wild beasts and then worried by dogs until they expired; and others dressed in shirts made stiff with wax, fixed to axletrees, and set on fire in his gardens in order to illuminate them. This persecution was general throughout the whole Roman Empire."[59] J. C. Ryle states, "Let it never surprise true Christians if they are slandered and misrepresented in this world. They must not expect to fare better than their Lord. Let them rather look forward to it as a matter of course and see in it a part of the cross which all must bear after conversion. Lies and false reports are among Satan's choicest weapons. When he cannot deter men from serving Christ, he labors to harass them and make Christ's service uncomfortable. Let us bear it patiently and not count it a strange thing. The words of the Lord Jesus should often come to our minds: 'Woe unto you, when all men shall speak well of you' (Luke 6:26), and, 'Blessed are ye, when men shall revile you, and persecute you, and say all manner of evil against you falsely, for my sake'" (Matthew 5:11).[60]

It was false witnesses (lies) that led to Jesus' crucifixion. The Bible says that Satan is the wellspring of lies, the originating source of all falsehood and deception (John 8:44). "When the spider would attack thee, it extends its web to entangle thee."[61] It is a precarious and perilous web (maliciousness, slander, defamation) that enemies of the Cross use to weave the thread of falsehood. Spurgeon says, "Nothing baffles opponents like integrity, truthfulness, and holiness; they long to speak against you but cannot find a fair opportunity."[62] See Daniel 6:4. He continues, "God had a Son that had no fault, but He never had a son that was not found fault with. God Himself was slandered in paradise by Satan. Let us not expect, therefore, to escape from the venomous tongue."[63] John Bunyan said, "Therefore, I bind these lies and slanderous accusations to my person as an ornament. It belongs to my Christian profession to be vilified, slandered, reproached and reviled; and since all this is nothing but that, as God and my conscience testify, I rejoice in being reproached for Christ's sake."[64]

> Failure to cooperate with evil triggers the protest of evil. Evil threatened always reciprocates.

Persecution arises out of protest of that which is wrong and evil (that which is counter to biblical values, beliefs and practice). Failure to cooperate with evil triggers the protest of evil. Evil threatened always reciprocates. To protest against abortion, homosexuality, same-sex marriage, sex-slave trade, infanticide, genocide, pornography, gambling, substance abuse, and other immoral and deviant behavior excites hostile acts toward the Christian. To be unbending on that which is right and wrong is to always cross swords with the world. W. A. Criswell well said, "There is no such a thing as relative truth, and there is no such thing as situation ethics—that is, something might be right today, permissively, that was wrong yesterday. There is no such thing as that in the Word of God. What was right yesterday is right today and is right forever, for righteousness and morality are grounded in the person of Almighty God. It is never what a man says it is. It is never what a legislature says it is. It is never what a judge will define it to be. Righteousness and morality are reflections of the being of God, and God never changes. Right is forever right, and wrong is forever wrong, because that is God!"[65]

Persecution arises from a life that is oriented (aligned) completely "for Christ's sake." Says a great puritan writer, "There is in the life of every Christian a convicting light which shows the deformity of the works of darkness, and a piercing heat which searches the ungodly and troubles their conscience. This they cannot endure, and hence there rises in them a contrary fire of wicked hatred, and out of this the fiery trials of the godly." R. T. France says to be persecuted "indicates a whole orientation of life towards God and His will. Such a life is conspicuous and so attracts persecution."[66] "Manifesting "light" for righteousness in darkness exposes wrong politically, religiously and culturally, which prompts potential persecution (Matthew 5:14). Jesus said, "For every wrongdoer hates the Light, and does not come to the Light [but shrinks from it] for fear that his [sinful, worthless] activities will be exposed and condemned" (John 3:20 AMP). It's the believer who walks in the "Light" that reveals and disturbs things in the "dark." H. A. Ironside remarks, "The denial of His Name is the increasing apostasy around us on every hand. Those who have not denied His Name refuse all fellowship with this God-dishonoring condition of things. Christ is to them more precious than all else; even for the sake of service, they refuse to link themselves with that which dishonors or blasphemes that worthy name whereby they are called."[67] And this brings conflict with the world.

Persecution arises out of the believers' "narrow-mindedness" in advocating that Jesus is the only means to salvation and Heaven (Acts 4:12 and John 14:6). Persecution arises from misunderstanding or ignorance about Christian terms and worship. "The early church was accused of incest, cannibalism, treason, and atheism."[68]

Persecution arises out of jeopardy of monetary gain. William Barclay says, "When Christianity came to Ephesus, the trade of the silversmiths was dealt a mortal blow, for far fewer desired to buy the images which they fashioned (Acts 19:24–27). Christianity preaches a view of man which no totalitarian state can accept. Christianity deliberately aims to obliterate certain trades and professions and ways of making money. It still does—and therefore the Christian is still liable to persecution for his faith."[69]

Persecution arises out of repugnance to the Word of God itself. The Bible defines truth (John 17:17), and it's that truth that is opposed by the ungodly. Diocletian ordered the Scriptures to be burned at Nicomedia (February 23, 303). Jonathan Edwards says, "It is the Sword of the Spirit that pierces [Satan] and conquers him. It is that great and strong sword with which God punishes Leviathan, that crooked serpent. It is that sharp sword that proceeds out of the mouth of Him who sat on the horse, with which He smites his enemies. Every text is a dart to torment the old serpent. He has felt the stinging smart thousands of times. Therefore, he is engaged against the Bible and hates every word of it."[70] "Sink the Bible," says Henry Ward Beecher, "to the bottom of the ocean, and still man's obligations to God would be unchanged. He would have the same path to tread, only his lamp and guide would be gone; the same voyage to make, but his chart and compass would be overboard!"[71]

But its root cause is hostile, antagonistic opposition to Christ (John 15:18). The real target in persecution is Christ. Paul says, "For many walk, of whom I have told you often, and now tell you even weeping, that they are the enemies of the cross of Christ" (Philippians 3:18). Matthew Henry states, "Whatever pretense persecutors have, it is the power of godliness that they have an enmity to; it is really Christ and His righteousness that are maligned, hated, and persecuted. For Thy sake I have borne reproach" (Psalm 69:9; Romans 8:36). Chafer says, "The believer is the object of the Satanic attack because of the great fact that unto him is committed the great ministry of reconciliation; that by his testimony both in life and word, and by his prayers, the facts of redemption may be given to the world; and if Satan can but cripple [and I add, crush through persecution] the believer's service, he accomplishes much in resisting the present purpose of God."[72]

J. C. Macaulay put it well: "If the world had nothing better than a Cross for Jesus, it will not have a royal carriage for His followers; if only thorns for Him, there will not be garlands for us....Only let us see that the world's hatred of us is really 'for Christ's sake' and not on account of anything hateful in us and unworthy of the gracious Lord whom we represent."[73]

When pain and anguish seize me, Lord,
All my support is from Thy Word.
My soul dissolves for heaviness;
Uphold me with Thy strengthening grace.

The proud have framed their scoffs and lies.
They watch my feet with envious eyes
And tempt my soul to snares and sin,
Yet Thy commands I ne'er decline.

They hate me, Lord, without a cause.
They hate to see me love Thy laws,
But I will trust and fear Thy name
Till pride and malice die with shame.

~ Isaac Watts (1719)

6
Criminality of Persecution

"Jesus is persecuted in every injured saint, and He is mighty to avenge His beloved ones."[74]

~ C. H. Spurgeon

"Saul of Tarsus," writes Swindoll, "hated the name of Jesus. So much so, he became a self-avowed, violent aggressor, persecuting and killing Christians in allegiance to the God of Heaven."[75] It was this cruel persecutor of Christians that Christ asked, "Why persecutest thou me?" (Acts 9:4). Matthew Henry explains, "He (Saul of Tarsus) thought he was persecuting only a company of poor, weak, silly people that were an offence and eyesore to the Pharisees, little imagining that there was one in Heaven that he was all this while insulting. Note, those who persecute the saints persecute Christ Himself, and He takes what is done against them as done against Himself, and accordingly will be the judgment in the great day."[76]

It is no small matter to persecute Christians, for nothing engenders the wrath and displeasure of God any more severely. The Bible says, "God is just: He will pay back trouble to those who trouble you and give relief to you who are troubled, and to us as well. This will happen when the Lord Jesus is revealed from heaven in blazing fire with his powerful angels" (2 Thessalonians 1:6–7 NIV). The troublers are to be troubled. Some now; all hereafter. Jesus said of such "troublers": "If he were thrown into the sea with a huge rock tied to his neck, he would be far better *off than facing the punishment in store* for those who harm these little children's souls. I am warning you!" (Luke 17:2–3 TLB). The writer of Hebrews says, "It is *a fearful thing* to fall into the hands of the living God" (Hebrews 10:31). The Lord says, "Touch not mine anointed, and do my prophets no harm" (Psalm 105:15). "Anointed" applies to those consecrated to God's service and at times to His covenant people (Psalm 89:38 and Psalm 89:51). Harrell says: "God has all the ages in which to demonstrate his justice…for they [ungodly] carry in themselves 'the germs of certain ruin.'"[77] Christ has such an affinity with His people that what is done to them is, in essence, done to Him.

The wicked had better realize that to touch the righteous is extremely dangerous and hazardous. "For he that toucheth you toucheth the apple of his eye" (Zechariah 2:8). John Calvin elucidates, "God will protect us as the apple of his eye" (Psalm 17:8). As then [with David who spoke the words] the Holy Spirit has elsewhere used this similitude, so I am disposed to regard this passage as intimating that the love of God towards the faithful is so tender that when they are hurt, He burns with so much displeasure, as though one attempted to pierce His eyes. For God cannot otherwise set forth how much and how ardently He loves us and how careful He is of our salvation than by comparing us to the apple of His eye. There is nothing, as we know, more delicate or more tender than this is in the body of man; for were one to bite my finger or prick my arm or my legs or even severely to would me, I should feel no such pain as by having my eye or the pupil of my eye injured. God then by this solemn message declares that the Church is to Him like the apple of His eye so that He can by no means bear it to be hurt or touched."[78]

> I love Thy church, O God;
>> Her walls before Thee stand
> Dear as the apple of Thine eye
>> And graven on Thy hand.
>> ~ Timothy Dwight, grandson of Jonathan Edwards (1800)

John MacArthur states, "Vindication and retribution are to be exercised by God, not man, in matters of spiritual persecution (Deuteronomy 32:35; Proverbs 25:21, 22; Romans 12:19–21; 1 Thessalonians 5:15; Revelation 19:2). When God repays and how God repays are to be determined by Him."[79] But repay He will! God will set things right. See 2 Thessalonians 1:6. The dogs lapped up Ahab's blood where Naboth was murdered (1 Kings 21:19). Haman was hung on the gallows he erected for Mordecai (Esther 7:10). Shadrach, Meshach and Abednego survived the fiery furnace, whereas the soldiers that thrust them into it were slain by its intense heat (Daniel 3:22). The infidels and idolatrous young men that mocked the prophet Elisha were mauled by two female bears (2 Kings 2:23–24).

"Many that despise and persecute God's saints and ministers when they are living," writes Matthew Henry, "would be glad to have them again when they are gone. 'Send Lazarus to me, and send Lazarus to my father's house.' We never read of Saul's going to Samuel to consult him in any of the difficulties he was in....[T]hen he slighted him and perhaps hated him. But now that he is dead, 'Oh, for Samuel again! By all means, bring me up Samuel' (1 Samuel 28:11)."[80] A torch for righteousness and justice is extinguished with each saint's martyrdom (or death by other means) that does not go unnoticed (their absence makes the darkness darker) even by the ungodly (Matthew 5:14). With the extraction of the *salt of the earth* (Christians), the world loses its source of preservation from corruption and wickedness (Matthew 5:13).

To all that have persecuted the saints out of hatred, ignorance, spiritual blindness, or political or religious pressure (as Paul did) gracious mercy and forgiveness await at the throne of God. See Acts 9:1–19 and Ephesians 2:4. Mostafa, Egyptian Christian (convert from Islam) and modern day "Paul," testifies to the availability of salvation to all that call on Christ. She said, "I planned to kill my cousin, your [God's] follower. But now I am prepared to give my life for You myself."[81] Converted persecutors become Heaven's best advocates. Just ask Paul.

> Oh, that at last by love compelled
> The rebels might submit,
> In humble hope of mercy yield
> And tremble at Thy feet;
>
> The faith they persecute, embrace;
> On Thee their Lord rely;
> And live the monuments of Thy grace
> And for Thy glory die!
>
> ~ Charles Wesley (1744)

7
Cost of Discipleship

"Sit down, therefore, I beseech you, and seriously count the cost and ask yourselves again and again whether you count all things but dung and dross and are willing to suffer the loss of all things so that you may win Christ and be found in Him."[82]

~ George Whitefield

Billy Graham said that we have lost the meaning of discipleship—of what it really means to follow Jesus Christ.[83] All are told to count the cost prior to becoming a follower of Christ. In Matthew 16:24, Jesus says, "If anyone wishes to follow Me [as My disciple], he must deny himself [set aside selfish interests], and take up his cross [expressing a willingness to endure whatever may come] and follow Me [believing in Me, conforming to My example in living and, if need be, suffering or perhaps dying because of faith in Me]" (AMP). That is, count the cost to bear the Cross. Dietrich Bonhoeffer said, "When Christ calls a man, he bids him come and die."[84] Arthur Pink elucidates, "At the outset of the Christian life, we are bidden to first sit down and 'count the cost' (Luke 14:28), which means that we are required to contemplate those sufferings which the following of Christ is likely to involve, and it is well that we should frequently remind ourselves that 'we must through much tribulation enter into the kingdom of God' (Acts 14:22). It is criminal silence on the part of any servant of God to conceal from his hearers that a true profession of the name of Christ will necessarily bring down upon us not only the scorn and opposition of the outside world, but also the hatred and persecution of the false religious world. "Beloved, think it not strange concerning the fiery trial which is to try you, as though some strange thing happened unto you' (1 Peter 4:12)."[85]

John MacArthur, commenting on Luke 10:38 ("he that taketh not his cross, and followeth after me, is not worthy of me"), states, "Here is Jesus' first mention of the word 'cross' to His disciples. To them it would have evoked a picture of a violent, degrading death. He was demanding total commitment from them—even unto physical death—and making this call to full surrender a part of the message they were to proclaim to others. This same call to life-or-death devotion to Christ is repeated in Matthew 16:24; Mark 8:34; Luke 9:23; 14:27."[86] Hudson Taylor wrote, "Carrying the cross *does mean* following in Jesus' footsteps. And in His footsteps are rejection, broken heartedness, persecution and death. There are not two Christ's—an easy-going one for easy-going Christians, and a suffering one for exceptional believers. There is only one Christ."[87] See 1 Peter 2:21. "The cross means sharing the suffering of Christ," writes Bonhoeffer, "to the last and to the fullest. Every Christian has his own cross waiting for him, a cross destined and designed by God. Each must endure his allotted share of suffering and rejection. But each has a different share."[88] Christ's feet suffered in the furnace and even so must His children's (Revelation 1:15). Jon Courson states, "Taking up your cross means that you identify with Jesus to the point of suffering and shame, rejection, and perhaps even death. Taking up your cross is something you choose to do, not something you put up with. It's a choice to deny yourself, a determination that, no matter what, you'll stand for Jesus."[89]

> Jesus, I my cross have taken,
>   All to leave and follow thee;
> Destitute, despised, forsaken,
>   Thou from hence my all shalt be.
>
> ~ Henry Francis Lyte (1825)

Bearing the cross involves great cost.

Bearing the cross involves great cost. "Once upon a time," states John Piper, "there was a safe, private place to take your controversial stand for Jesus. No more. If you are going to stand, you will be shot at—either figuratively or literally."[90] Just ask Masih, a Hindu convert. She testifies, "My family and friends asked me to renounce Christ. When I didn't, much persecution followed, and my life was in danger. I had to flee."[91]

John Owens, referencing the cruel torture of biblical saints recorded in Hebrews 11, said, "All the evils here enumerated did befall the persons intended on the account of their faith and the profession thereof. The apostle does not present unto the Hebrews a company of miserable, distressed creatures that fell into that state through their own default or merely on the account of a common providence disposing their lot in this world into such a state of misery, as it is with many; but all the things mentioned, they underwent merely and solely on the account of their faith in God and the profession of true religion, so as that their *case differed in nothing from that which they might be called unto.*"[92]

The first-century church understood that part and parcel of being a disciple of Christ was persecution ("take up your cross and follow me") and willingly endured it. "Dragged crosses are very heavy, but carried crosses are very light."[93] This Paul made crystal clear to Timothy, "Yea, and all that will live godly in Christ Jesus *shall suffer* persecution" (2 Timothy 3:12). However, many in the church today have failed to make the inseparable connection. As T. Manson says, "Carnal fancy imagineth a path strewed with lilies and roses; we are too tenderfooted to think of briars and thorns."[94] And therefore, saints faint in the wake of persecution.

> Tell me not of gain or loss,
>   Ease, enjoyment, pomp, and power,
> Welcome poverty and cross,
>   Shame, reproach, affliction's hour.
> "Follow me!"—I know the voice;
>   Jesus, Lord, Thy steps I see.
> Now I take Thy yoke by choice,
>   Light Thy burden now to me.
>
> ~ James Montgomery (1825)

To summarize: Discipleship, Graham said, costs everything, a commitment to serve Christ without reservation. It says, I am willing to follow Him even to physical death if that's what He wants me to do.[95] True discipleship echoes the great words of Ittai the Gittite, concerning David, "As the LORD liveth, and as my Lord the king liveth, surely in what place my Lord the king shall be, whether in death or life, even there also will thy servant be" (2 Samuel 15:21). Robert Murray M'Cheyne said, "If you will bear the cross, it will bear you."[96]

> Must Jesus bear the cross alone
> And all the world go free?
> No, there's a cross for ev'ry one,
> And there's a cross for me.
>
> The consecrated cross I'll bear
> Till death shall set me free,
> And then go home my crown to wear,
> For there's a crown for me.
>
> O precious cross! O glorious crown!
> O resurrection day!
> Ye angels, from the stars come down
> And bear my soul away.
>
> ~ Thomas Shepherd (1693)

S. D. Gordon shares a challenging story about counting the cost of discipleship. A Hindu asked a Salvation Army officer the meaning of the phrase "sell whatsoever thou hast." Despite the man's desire to be a Christian, he was unwilling to meet that condition of salvation (dispose of whatever might stand in the way of being a follower of Christ). Later, at a Salvation Army meeting, he started forward to be saved, when men entered, seized him and forcibly took him away to the terror of all gathered.

Several weeks later the young man returned, saying, "I have begun to sell all." At that time, he gave testimony of God's dealing in his life. A Bible was placed into his hands and the Holy Spirit made a great appeal for salvation. However, he was haunted by the words "sell whatsoever thou hast," words which he came to understand. His family were wealthy and connected to heathen temple worship and sought to dissuade him from becoming a Christian. Finding their efforts futile, they kept watch on him, and when he went to the Salvationist meeting to profess Christ, they had him forcibly removed. He was imprisoned, chained hand and foot, and poorly fed in efforts to dissuade him from following Christ, but all to no avail. Upon escaping the prison, he came to the only Christian place he knew, the Salvation Army, and asked to be helped and housed. Two weeks later the man disappeared, but after some days he returned. He had been taken to the heathen god's holy city and forced to bathe in the Ganges. "But," he said, "as I stood in the water of the Ganges, I said, 'Lord Jesus, wash me in Thy precious blood,' and when I was forced to bow to idols, I bowed my soul to the eternal Father and said, 'Thou art God alone.'" He refused the pleas from parents, brothers, sisters, and tutor to denounce Christ.

"Well," the Salvationist told him, "now you know the meaning of 'sell whatsoever thou hast.'"

"Not yet," he said, "but I have sold nearly all." Upon saying that, he left again. When he returned, grief-stricken, he said, "I have sold all. I have not only ceased to be a Brahmin (to embrace Hinduism); I have ceased to be a human being. I am not only an outcast; I am dead. I have neither father, mother, brothers, nor sisters. I have been burned in effigy and the ashes buried. It was not the effigy they burned; it was I. My father would not recognize me now if he met me on the street, nor would my mother. I am dead. I have been buried. It is the end. I have sold all."

The young man had counted the cost of being Christ's disciple and though it was great and grievous, chose to follow Him. "The rich young Jew to whom the words were first spoken saw things bigger than Jesus; the rich young Hindu saw Jesus bigger than things. Each held to what he prized most and let the other go. Would it not be better if we were to count the cost and then deliberately decide and if it be to follow, then follow all the way?[97]

8
Motivation for Suffering Persecution

"Discipleship means allegiance to the suffering Christ, and it is therefore not at all surprising that Christians should be called upon to suffer. In fact, it is a joy and a token of his grace."[98]
~ Dietrich Bonhoeffer

"For unto you it is given in the behalf of Christ, not only to believe on him, but also to suffer for his sake" (Philippians 1:29). Motives underlie actions. The Christian's all-encompassing motive to bear persecution is "for Christ's sake." Why is it a privilege to suffer for "Christ's sake"? To suffer for Christ identifies the saint in an intimate way with the suffering that Christ bore at Calvary. Paul longed (as all believers should) to share in the suffering of Christ (Philippians 3:10). Albert Barnes states, "Paul wished to be just like his Savior. He felt that it was an honor to live as He did, to evince the spirit that He did and to suffer in the same manner. The idea is that it is an honor to suffer as Christ suffered and that the true Christian will esteem it a privilege to be made just like Him, not only in glory, but in trial."[99]

To suffer for Christ demonstrates the degree of love possessed for Him (John 14:15; Matthew 22:37; John 15:13). Charles Finney says, "Christ was persecuted unto death for our sakes. It was for us—that 'by His stripes, we might be healed.' Then He stood up for us when there was no other eye that would pity and no arm but His that could save. So great was His love that He enjoyed it. We are told it was 'for the joy set before Him that He endured the cross, despising the shame.' This was not the joy of a personal salvation, but the joy of saving others. So far as the same sort of love animates our service for Him and His people now, so far we shall certainly enjoy this life."[100] To suffer for Christ manifests to the world our allegiance to Him whatever the cost or consequence (Luke 9:23). William Secker says, "Neither the persecuting hand of men nor the chastising hand of God relaxed ancient singular saints. Believers resemble the moon, which emerges from her eclipse by keeping her motion and ceases not to shine because the dogs bark at her. Shall we cease to be professors because others will not cease to be persecutors?"[101]

> A charge to keep I have,
>   A God to glorify,
> A never dying soul to save
>   And fit it for the sky.
>
> To serve the present age,
>   My calling to fulfill,
> Oh, may it all my pow'rs engage
>   To do my Master's will!
>
> Arm me with jealous care
>   As in Thy sight to live,
> And now Thy servant, Lord, prepare
>   A strict account to give!
>
> Help me to watch and pray
>   And still on Thee rely;
> Oh, let me not my trust betray
>   But press to realms on high.
>
> ~ Charles Wesley (1762)

When communist authorities threatened Romanian Baptist pastor Josef Tson in 1977 for preaching the Gospel, the pastor famously quipped, "Don't you understand that when you kill me you send me to Glory? You cannot threaten me with Glory. The more suffering, the more troubles, the greater the glory. So, why say, 'Stop this trouble'? Because the more [suffering], the greater the glory up there."[102]

To suffer for Christ plants seeds of righteousness to further the cause of Christ. To this Paul testifies: "But part of my work is to suffer for you; and I am glad, for I am helping to finish up the remainder of Christ's sufferings for his body, the Church" (Colossians 1:24 TLB). Criswell says, "The sufferings of Paul do not add to the finished work of redemption [Christ's redemptive work at Calvary has no deficiency and is 'finished'] but are incurred in making known the redeeming work of Christ to the Gentiles."[103] The afflictions of the believer supplement, not in atonement or justification of the sinner, but the extension of the message of redemption, to the entire world. That is, the believer must extend the message of Christ's suffering to the world (its who, what and why) by suffering physically for Christ; through persecution Christ's mission and message are maximized and magnified.

> The afflictions of the believer supplement, not in atonement or justification of the sinner, but the extension of the message of redemption, to the entire world.

With the saints' suffering, the church and kingdom of God flourish; without it, they are famished. How do Christ's sufferings arrive at your school, workplace, house or senate chamber, city and community? It's through the afflictions of the believer (Colossians 1:24). How is the message of Calvary to break through to the more than ten million unreached people groups of the world? It will only happen through suffering "for Christ's sake." John Piper emphatically says, "There never has been a breakthrough into an unreached place or people without suffering. If you're going to be a missionary, mark it down—pain, loss of a child, malaria, marital strife, tensions on the team, demonic opposition, martyrdom. It's going to come. Don't think it's strange when it comes. It's the price. He paid His life for our salvation. We join Him in that suffering to display the nature of it."[104]

To suffer for Christ magnifies His holy person and position. To suffer for Christ verifies salvation. To suffer for Christ shows that we are being faithful to our confession and conviction and it shows in our conduct. Of the early apostles the Bible says, "And they departed from the presence of the council, rejoicing that they were counted worthy to suffer shame for his name" (Acts 5:41). To the apostles it was a matter of great joy and honor to be counted fit by the Jewish council to make them suffer for "Christ's sake."

To suffer for Christ pleases Him. See Galatians 1:10. In *Octavius,* Felix Menucius said, "It's a beautiful thing to God when a Christian does battle with pain. When he faces threats, punishments, and tortures by mocking death and treading underfoot the horror of the executioner; when he raises up his freedom in Christ as the standard before kings and princes; when he yields to God alone and, triumphant and victorious, he tramples upon the very man who has pronounced sentence upon him. God finds all these things beautiful."[105]

To suffer for Christ is a sheer honor. During the reign of Queen Mary, a Christian imprisoned for "Christ's sake" wrote to a friend: "A prisoner for Christ! What is this for a poor worm! Such honor have not all the saints. Both the degrees which I took at the university have not set me so high as the honor of becoming a prisoner of the Lord."[106] "When under sentence of death, good Bishop Ridley wrote thus to his relatives: 'I warn you all, my beloved kinsfolk, that ye be not amazed or astonished at the kind of my departure or dissolution; for I assure you I think it the most honor that ever I was called unto in all my life. And therefore, I thank God heartily for it, that it hath pleased Him to call me, of His great mercy, unto this high honor, to suffer death willingly for His sake and in His cause; unto the which honor He called the holy prophets and His dearly beloved apostles and His blessed chosen martyrs.'"[107]

Therefore, with James I say, "Consider it all joy, my brothers and sisters, when you encounter various trials" (James 1:2 NASB).

9
The Rejoice Part of Persecution

"How did Jesus expect His disciples to react under persecution? We are not to retaliate like an unbeliever, nor sulk like a child, nor lick our wound in self-pity like a dog, nor just grin and bear it like a Stoic, still less pretend we enjoy it like a masochist. What then? We are to rejoice as a Christian should and even 'leap for joy'" (Luke 6:23)."[108]

~ John Stott

D. L. Moody said, "Joy flows right on through trouble; joy flows on through the dark; joy flows in the night as well as in the day; joy flows all through persecution and opposition."[109] "Rejoice and be exceeding glad, for great is your reward in Heaven" (Matthew 5:12). The expressions *rejoice* and *be exceeding glad* are terms Jesus uses to describe the joy of the saints at the marriage of the Lamb (Revelation 19:7).[110] Jesus is saying, "Rejoice in persecution for Me, as you will in celebration when with Me." "Rejoice" means to be happy, to receive with pleasure that which is experienced, and gladness.[111]

"Rejoice" is reinforced with the word "glad" which means "to experience a state of great joy and gladness, often involving verbal expression and appropriate body movement—"to be extremely joyful, to be overjoyed, to rejoice greatly."[112] See 1 Peter 1:6 and 4:13. Matthew Henry says, "It is not enough to be patient and content under these sufferings [persecution] as under common afflictions and not to render railing for railing; but we must rejoice, because the honor and dignity, the pleasure and advantage, of suffering for Christ are much more considerable than the pain or shame of it."[113] Howard remarks, "The believer should respond in joy to the occasion of suffering, because it is by means of testing that the ultimate goal of spiritual maturity is accomplished (James 1:2–4). Furthermore, only by faith in God is such a response possible (James 1:6)."[114] However, the superior reason believers are to rejoice when oppressed is that they are allowed to some degree to imitate the suffering (example) of Christ (He was scourged, reviled, slandered, ridiculed, rejected, crucified). See Philippians 3:10.

Bloomberg says, "Because this life is just a fraction of all eternity, we can and must rejoice even in persecution. The joy commanded here, as elsewhere in scripture (James 1:2), is not an emotion but an attitude."[115] Calvin states, "The meaning is, a remedy is at hand, that we may not be overwhelmed by unjust reproaches; for, as soon as we raise our minds to Heaven, we there behold vast grounds of joy, which dispel sadness."[116] "Far from being despondent and depressed," states Leon Morris, "saddened or enraged, Christians who find themselves in this situation [persecution] are bidden, 'Rejoice.'"[117] In this the disciples serve as our example (Acts 5:41–42).

"Reward" means "God will reward you richly."[118] Therefore, Christ is saying, "Leap and shout for joy" upon being persecuted (when deplorable, demeaning, and detestable things are spoken about you; cruel and brutal acts are inflicted upon you and/or to family and friends), knowing that your awaiting reward in Heaven is not meager or insignificant but "great" (transcends vastly the suffering endured). Keep in mind, "The sufferings of this present time are not worthy to be compared with the glory which shall be revealed in us" (Romans 8:18). (See Chapter 11: *The Crown of Life.*)

Avoid pride in persecution (that spoils all), but take pleasure in them, as Paul did (2 Corinthians 12:10).[119]

10
Persecution Authenticates Profession

"Persecution has been the portion and the proof of the most eminent saints in all ages."[120]

~ Joseph Benson

Readiness to suffer religious persecution is a sign of saintliness and loyalty to God. Paul wrote, "All that will live godly in Christ Jesus shall suffer persecution" (2 Timothy 3:12). Suffering for Christ's sake affirms the believer's allegiance, love, and devotion to Christ. Arthur Pink well states, "Thus, it is by their godly living the true are distinguished from the false [mere professor], and by the opposition which they meet with from the latter, that they may be clearly identified."[121] Weber says, "Persecution by the king's enemies was one of the most significant marks of a kingdom servant."[122] John MacArthur comments, "Proof of the believer's ultimate glory is that he suffers—whether it comes as mockery, ridicule, or physical persecution—because of His Lord."[123] Again, MacArthur says, "People who profess to be Christians but never personally experience any antagonism from the world need to examine themselves."[124] See Romans 8:17.

Thomas à Kempis states, "If thou art willing to suffer no adversity, how wilt thou be the friend of Christ?"[125] Thomas Watson declared, "Persecution is the touchstone of sincerity. It discovers true saints from hypocrites. Unsound hearts look good in prosperity—but in time of persecution fall away (Matthew 13:20–21). Hypocrites cannot sail in stormy weather. They will follow Christ to Mount Olivet—but not to Mount Calvary."[126]

Persecution is a type of sifter or sieve that separates the sheep from the goats, the spiritual from the carnal. Spurgeon says, "There must be these fiery persecutions, that the drossy hypocrites may be purged out. Trial and temptation also discover the reality of conversion. Now the fact that he can stand against temptation is one of the very best evidences that he is born again and made a new creature in Christ Jesus, and those who see such a change confess that this is the finger of God."[127] He continues, "Persecution will try your love to Jesus. If you really love Him, you will cheerfully stand in the pillory of reproach with Him; and when enemies have filth to hurl, you will say, 'Throw it upon me rather than upon Him; if there is a hard thing to be said, say it about me rather than against my Lord.'"[128]

O Thou from whom all goodness flows,
    I lift my soul to Thee;
In all my sorrows, conflicts, woes,
    Good Lord, remember me.

When on my aching, burdened heart
    My sins lie heavily,
Thy pardon grant; new peace impart.
    Good Lord, remember me.

When trials sore obstruct my way
    And ills I cannot flee,
Oh, let my strength be as my day;
    Good Lord, remember me.

If, for Thy sake, upon my name
    Shame and reproach shall be,
All hail reproach and welcome shame!
    Good Lord, remember me.

If worn with pain, disease, or grief
    This feeble frame should be,
Grant patience, rest, and kind relief;
    Good Lord, remember me.

When in the solemn hour of death,
    I wait Thy just decree,
Be this the prayer of my last breath:
    Good Lord, remember me.

~ Thomas Haweis (1791)

11
The Crown of Life

"To those who suffer most, God imparts the highest rewards. Hence, the crown of martyrdom has been thought to be the brightest that any of the redeemed shall wear."[129]

~ Albert Barnes

Richard Baxter said, "If there be glory laid up for them that die *in* the Lord, much more shall they be glorified that die *for* the Lord."[130] "Be faithful, even to the point of death, and I will give you life as your victor's crown" (Revelation 2:10 NIV). Says Spurgeon, "Remember, the rougher the road the sweeter the rest, and the greater the suffering the brighter the crown at the last. Those who have to bear most for Jesus will be those to whom He will most sweetly say, 'Well done, good and faithful servant, enter thou into the joy of thy Lord.'"[131]

God's goodness is showered upon the persecuted presently, but their full reward will be in Heaven.[132] What is the reward? Newman and Stine say, "It is a reward [compensation which is valuable and special] of God's grace, that is, a reward not merited but which God wills to give to those who serve Him faithfully. It is not a compensation for work done, but rather a gift which far exceeds any service rendered."[133] Saith Matthew Henry, "It is in Heaven, future, and out of sight; but well secured, out of the reach of chance, fraud, and violence. Note, God will provide that those who lose *for* Him, though it be life itself, shall not lose *by* Him in the end. Heaven, at last, will be an abundant recompence for all the difficulties we meet with in our way. This is that which has borne up the suffering saints in all ages."[134]

The "Victor's Crown" or "Crown of Life" (Revelation 2:10; 2 Timothy 4:8; James 1:12; 1 Peter 5:4) "is the garland, the mark of a conqueror, or of one rejoicing."[135] This incorruptible crown (permanent) is an allusion to the corruptible crown or wreath (temporary) that was awarded to the conquerors in the Olympic games in biblical times. At life's conclusion (end of the contest against Satan and evil), the believer that endured trials and tribulations faithfully to death will be honored with the "Crown of Life" (probably the highest of all distinctions) by Christ. Of this crown, Alexander Maclaren says that though the terms royalty, triumph, festal goodness all fused together are incomplete to describe it, they "are not useless symbols; may we experience their fulfilment!"[136] The future "hope" of receiving the Crown of Life renders present suffering, though grievous, endurable (James 1:12).

The believer's crown(s) (there are five potential crowns[137]) will determine their rank and role in Heaven. See Luke 19:11–27. "He [Christ] will determine the measure of our award by the degree of our fidelity (see Luke 19:17, 19). The more faithful and devoted the life on earth, the larger the recompense, the brighter the crown, the broader the sphere in the heavenly kingdom."[138] Whatever crown(s) that are received will be laid at Christ's feet. John writes, "And cast their crowns before the throne" (Revelation 4:10). Matthew Henry comments, "They gave God the glory of the holiness wherewith He had crowned their souls on earth and the honor and happiness with which He crowns them in Heaven. They owe all their graces and all their glories to Him and acknowledge that His crown is infinitely more glorious than theirs and that it is their glory to be glorifying God."[139]

> Upon the crystal pavement, down
> At Jesus' pierced feet,
> Joyful, I'll cast my golden crown
> And His dear name repeat.
>
> ~ Thomas Shepherd (1693)

What might the arrival scene be like for the faithful and persecuted saint in Heaven? Charles Simeon says, "Conceive of the saint as just entering into the eternal world and ascending to Heaven from the flames of martyrdom. What a cloud of witnesses come forth to congratulate him on his victory and to welcome him to those blest abodes! Behold him welcomed too by his Lord and Master for whose name he has suffered and under whose banners he has fought.

Hear the plaudit with which he is received: 'Well done, good and faithful servant; enter thou into the joy of thy Lord.' See the crown [the Crown of Life] brought forth and put upon his head, and behold him seated on the very throne of God Himself, according to that promise, 'To him that overcometh, will I give to sit with me in my throne, even as I also overcame, and am set down with my Father in his throne.'"[140]

This is why Paul said that this earthly suffering is not to be compared with the "shining-greatness that He is going to give us" (Romans 8:18 NLV). Spurgeon said, "And remember, though Simon had to bear the cross for a very little while, it gave him lasting honor. Even so the cross we carry is only for a little while at most, and then we shall receive the crown, the glory. Surely we should love the cross and, instead of shrinking from it, count it very dear, when it works out for us 'a far more exceeding and eternal weight of glory.'"[141]

> Stand up, my soul; shake off your fears
>   And gird the gospel armor on.
> March to the gates of endless joy,
>   Where your great Captain Savior's gone.
>
> Hell and your sins resist your course,
>   But Hell and sin are vanquished foes;
> Your Jesus nailed them to the cross
>   And sang the triumph when he rose.
>
> Then let my soul march boldly on,
>   Press forward to the heav'nly gate;
> There peace and joy eternal reign,
>   And glitt'ring robes for conqu'rors wait.
>
> There shall I wear a starry crown
>   And triumph in almighty grace,
> While all the armies of the skies
>   Join in my glorious Leader's praise.
>
>   ~ Isaac Watts (1707)

Spurgeon found great encouragement in the words of Jesus in Matthew 5:10–12. He was a London pastor who in his early thirties preached to 6,000 people on Sundays and whose printed sermons were distributed around the world. His biblical conservativism anguished liberals, which ignited their loud criticism (verbal/written attacks). Being human, at times the vicious verbal attacks spurred bouts of depression. Upon one such occasion, his wife printed two verses, Matthew 5:11–12, on large sheets of paper and adhered them on the ceiling above their bed. Every night and morning, as Spurgeon's eyes fixated on them, the expectation of future reward instilled new courage and determination not to quit, but to press on to the end.[142] May the same verses equally encourage us in times of persecution and despondency.

12
Cruelty of Persecutors

"No one makes us afraid, or leads us into captivity as we have set our faith on Jesus. For though we are beheaded, and crucified, and exposed to beasts and chains and fire and all other forms of torture, it is plain that we do not forsake the confession of our faith, but the more things of this kind which happen to us the more are their others who become believers…through the name of Jesus."[143]

~ Justin Martyr

John Henry Newman said, "The early Christians had to endure 'the shame' after their Master's pattern. They had to die in the midst of enemies who reviled them and in mockery bid them (as in Christ's case) come down from the cross. They were supported on no easy couch, soothed by no attentive friends."[144] The church at large fails to understand the violent and agonizing torture of persecuted saints, not only of yesterday, but of the present hour. The Bible says, "Others were tortured, not accepting deliverance; that they might obtain a better resurrection: And others had trial of cruel mockings and scourgings, yea, moreover of bonds and imprisonment: They were stoned, they were sawn asunder, were tempted, were slain with the sword: they wandered about in sheepskins and goatskins; being destitute, afflicted, tormented; (Of whom the world was not worthy:) they wandered in deserts, and in mountains, and in dens and caves of the earth" (Hebrews 11:35–38).

Tortured

A. W. Pink says, "The word 'torture' [tortured] here signifies 'were racked': those Old Testament saints were fastened to a device and then a wrench was turned which caused their joints to be pulled out of their sockets—a method of torture frequently resorted to by fiendish Romanists when seeking to force Protestants to recant. By this fearful form of suffering the graces of God's people were tested and tried."[145]

Trial of Cruel Mocking

Christians, for the faith, encountered and still encounter scorn, derision, and sneering. Samson endured such mocking from the Philistines (Judges 16:21, 25). And in the rebuilding of the walls about Jerusalem the Jews suffered likewise from Sanballat and Tobiah (Nehemiah 4:1–3).

Scourging

A rod or whip (later thongs of sharp points of iron or lead called "scorpions" were attached to the whip to inflict severer pain [1 Kings 12:11]) was used to flog the person upon his back as he laid on the ground (later times he was tied to a post).[146] Paul was beaten in this fashion five times (2 Corinthians 11:24). Preceding execution the person would experience scourging or whipping (flogging), as with Jesus (John 19:1). The disciples were forewarned that such persecution may be inflicted upon them (Matthew 23:34). Paul testifies prior to his conversion he inflicted this cruel punishment upon Christians (Acts 22:19).

Shackles and Imprisonment

The person imprisoned was placed in "stocks," an instrument of torture that forced the body into a twisted, distorted position. See Jeremiah 20:2. Albert Barnes gives description of "stocks" as used in the New Testament with regard to Paul and Silas: "The word 'stocks' with us denotes a machine made of two pieces of timber between which the feet of criminals are placed, and in which they are thus made secure. The account here does not imply necessarily that they were secured precisely in this way, but that they were fastened or secured by the feet, probably by cords, to a piece or beam of wood so that they could not escape. It is probable that the legs of the prisoners were bound to large pieces of wood which not only encumbered them, but which were so placed as to extend their feet to a considerable distance. In this condition it might be necessary for them to lie on their backs; and if this, as is probable, was on the cold ground, after their severe scourging, their sufferings must have been very great. Yet in the midst of this they sang praises to God."[147]

Stoned

Stoning was among the Jews' favorite methods of punishment. Stoning was not *always* purposed to kill the person, but sometimes simply to inflict great injury and pain (Mark 12:4). Naboth was stoned by the order of Ahab (1 Kings 21:13). Zachariah was stoned in the Lord's house (2 Chronicles 24:21). The prophets and other messengers of God were stoned (Matthew 23:37). Stephen was stoned to death (Acts 7:58–60). Paul was stoned at Lystra and presumed to be dead (Acts 14:19). An attempt by the Jews to stone Jesus failed (John 8:59).

Sawn Asunder

Perhaps the cruelest form of persecution is to be "sawn in twain." Epiphanius, in writing a discourse on Isaiah's life, states that he was *sawed asunder* with a wooden saw by orders of King Manasseh. Justin Martyr (*Dialogue with Trypho,* 120), Tertullian and Origen of Alexandria in their writings indicate the same. The apostle's inclusion of "sawn asunder" as a mode of persecution in Hebrews 11 might very well be a reference to Isaiah's death. Whether Isaiah died in this fashion the Bible doesn't say, but it appears very likely that he did. Albert Barnes says that to cut a person asunder was not an unusual form of punishment.[148]

Tempted

Tempted, in the context of Hebrews 11, may reference the believer's temptations to recant the faith to spare his life or that of family members. "It is very possible to conceive that this might have been among the highest aggravations of their sufferings."[149]

Slain with the Sword

King Saul ordered Doeg to slay with his sword 85 priests that sided with David (1 Samuel 22:18). The prophets of God were ordered slain with a sword by Jezebel (1 Kings 19:1–2).

Forced into Wandering

"They wandered in deserts, and in mountains, and in dens and caves of the earth." Driven from their homes and businesses by their persecutor, believers were forced to wear inferior clothing and live the life of the vagabond. A. W. Pink comments, "What a commentary upon fallen human nature: these saints of God were safer among the beasts of the field than in the religious world inflamed by the Devil! While these lines are being read, there are probably some of God's children in foreign lands suffering these very experiences."[150] Gouge says, "Saints had rather wander with a quiet conscience, holding the truth, than sit at ease in their own house under their own vines and fig trees with a torturing conscience upon denying the truth."[151]

Destitution

The saints were forced (either abandoned their possessions in escaping their persecutors or had them taken by them) to live without the "comforts" of life and survive on the bare necessities (poverty, without bodily food). They were spared death so that their misery and suffering could continue. See 1 Samuel 21:3 and 1 Kings 17:6. Matthew Henry states, "They had not raiment to put on, but were forced to cover themselves with the skins of slain beasts. They were driven out of all human society and forced to converse with the beasts of the field, to hide themselves in dens and caves and make their complaint to rocks and rivers, not more obdurate than their enemies. Such sufferings as these they endured then for their faith; and such they endured through the power of the grace of faith."[152]

Afflicted

Saints were vilified, maltreated, and greatly oppressed by evil men with evil means. A. W. Pink says, "'Afflicted' probably has reference to their state of mind: they were not emotionless stoics, but felt acutely their sad condition."[153]

Tormented

In their "wanderings" they were mistreated by unfriendly strangers that showed no concern or pity for their dire condition or needs.[154] Adam Clarke says they were "maltreated, harassed, variously persecuted by those to whom they brought the message of salvation."[155]

Additional Devices of Persecution Used to Inflict Pain upon Saints

The torturous treatment the world inflicts on the saint is inhumane, heartless, and barbaric, at its least. Simeon says, "It is scarcely to be conceived what sufferings men have inflicted on the people of God."[156]

Early martyrs (and some saints today), outside of being ostracized and discriminated against, have had their wealth and property pilfered, speech censored, and character defamed. They have experienced cruel tortures such as having nails placed in their shoes and being made to walk long distances, having fingernails removed, and having hands bound behind the back and feet in chains (sometimes for months or years) in unbearable prison conditions. Some have had nails hammered into their hands and been thrown into frozen lakes, dragged through the streets, and thrust into the den of lions. Others were burned at the stake, had teeth yanked or knocked out, were crucified or forced into sex slavery. These horrific and abominable forms of torture reveal the utter depravity (corruption) of man's heart and bitter hatred for God and make him worse than most savage beasts. "Note," states Matthew Henry, "there is no evil so black and horrid which, at one time or other, has not been said, falsely, of [or inflicted upon] Christ's disciples and followers."[157] And there is no pain infliction greater than that of watching one's spouse or children suffer torture. Perhaps this was part of Paul's reasoning for telling the unmarried, "It is good for them to remain single, as I am" (1 Corinthians 7:8 ESV). Paul was continually pressured to back down. One can only imagine what horrendous attacks Paul's wife and children would have received because of his biblical stance and declaration had he been married.

> There is no evil so black and horrid, which, at one time or other, has not been said, falsely, of [or inflicted upon] Christ's disciples and followers.
> Matthew Henry

Nero set Christians afire to use as torches to light his gardens. He sewed them in the skins of animals and allowed his hunting dogs to devour them. Hissing molten lead was poured upon them; red hot plates were affixed to the most sensitive parts of their bodies; eyes were yanked out; they were scraped with pincers; various parts of their bodies were cut off and roasted in front of them; and their hands and feet, while burning, had cold water poured over them to prolong the agony.[158]

History states that some tyrants, in thirst for greater forms of cruelty to inflict upon the saints, hired men to invent even more sadistic and atrocious instruments of torture.[159] Phalaris, (died 554 B.C.), tyrant of Akragas, is infamous for such cruelty. He had constructed a brass bull, hollowed inside, with a door in one side. Once the inward chamber was heated red hot with blazing fire, men would be placed in it and burned to death mercilessly (their cries representing the animal's bellowing).[160] The Romans were reported to have used this torture device to kill some Christians.[161] Similar inventions were devised by other tyrants.[162]

Such horrific and inhuman torture is what Christians prepared for in the first church, and to greater or lesser degree since. It is unknown what we may yet be called upon to endure for Christ's sake. But we know that whether it be persecution by the meanest of men and severest of methods or a lighter affliction, God will enable us to withstand the suffering and "glory in the tribulation," as He did the saints of old.

13
Reaction to Persecution

"We cannot say this or that trouble shall not befall, yet we may, by help of the Spirit, say, nothing that doth befall shall make me do that which is unworthy of a Christian."[163]
~ *Richard Sibbes*

In Matthew 10 Jesus reveals the biblical reaction of the sheep (persecuted saint) to the attack of the wolves (persecutors). He said, "Behold, I send you forth as sheep in the midst of wolves: be ye therefore wise as serpents, and harmless as doves. But beware of men: for they will deliver you up to the councils, and they will scourge you in their synagogues" (Matthew 10:16–17). Sheep picture innocence and blamelessness (Christians) and wolves indicate predators ("a person who is particularly vicious and dangerous—'vicious person, fierce wolf, fierce person.'"[164]).

Christians (sheep) are prey to and vulnerable to the vicious wolves of religious intolerance and antagonism for Christ and His teachings (Holy Scriptures). Some of the fiercest opposition arises from "within the camp." "If you resolve," states Arthur Pink, "that by divine grace you will 'live godly in Christ Jesus,' then know you that 'persecution' must be your portion. And that persecution will come upon you not from atheists and infidels—but from those bearing the name of Christians. It will issue from those who still keep up a 'form (or semblance) of godliness,' but who are strangers to its living power. It will come to you from empty professors whose compromising ways are condemned by your refusal to conform thereto, whose worldliness and carnality are rebuked by your spirituality. It was the religious leaders of Israel who hounded the Savior to His death!"[165]

The Christian's recourse to facing "wolves" is to act "wise" (shrewdness, skillfulness, and cunningness) as a snake. No animal equals snakes in their quickness and cleverness in escaping danger.[166] Therefore, Jesus says, imitate them in evading maltreatment.

Second, snakes have the ability (wisdom) to remain still and quiet, hidden from their predators for just the right moment to strike.[167] In battling the forces of unrighteousness, there is a time to speak and a time to be silent, of exposure and of concealment, which require godly wisdom to discern when which is appropriate.

Bruner says, "If we are to be sheep among wolves—and this is Jesus' intention—then we should at least be smart sheep, sheep who use our heads, sheep who don't overestimate the benevolence of wolves."[168] Simeon states, "It is lamentable to see how often well-meaning Christians defeat their own purposes by their want of judgment. They will reprove sin; but they will reprove it with so much harshness, or in so public a manner, as to irritate only, and not to reclaim, the offender. In conveying instruction also, they overlook all the circumstances of time and place, as well as the state of those they address. They forget that there is much wisdom required 'to win souls'; that they should 'choose out acceptable words,' which shall 'distil as the dew' and insinuate themselves gently into the minds of the hearers. They will speak the truth freely at all times without considering whether they be not 'casting their pearls before swine, who will only turn again and rend them.'"[169]

Third, snakes are cunning and savvy in attacking their prey. Cunningly devised schemes are enacted by the "serpents" of the world to persecute the religious. It was so with Daniel. Envy of Daniel's position above all government officials (except the king) prompted the leaders to plot a scheme (Ephesians 6:11) to remove him from office (Daniel 6:4). Unable to impeach him on grounds of wrongdoing, they contrived a plan to unseat him based on his religious habit of prayer. In the name of government reform or social injustice, sometimes legislation is passed that is nothing less than an underhanded, devious method to silence the voices of the righteous (discriminatory persecution). See Nehemiah 6:5–8. Cyprian cautions, "It is not persecution alone that we ought to fear, not those forces that in open warfare range abroad to overthrow and defeat the servants of God. It is easy enough to be on one's guard when the danger is obvious; one can stir up one's courage for the fight when the Enemy shows himself in his true colors. There is more need to fear and beware of the Enemy when he creeps up secretly, when he beguiles us by a show of peace and steals forward by those hidden approaches which have earned him the name of the 'Serpent.'"[170]

To summarize, the first part of Jesus' instruction about handling persecution was His saying that for the disciples (and every believer) to combat it successfully (not necessarily escape it but perhaps lessen it) demands divine wisdom, discernment of its devious schemes, continual anticipation of its occurrence and avoiding it whenever feasible (without jeopardizing the message or mission), discretionary speech (verbiage and its tone) and dependence upon Him (the Shepherd that cares for His sheep).

And harmless as doves. The Christian's demeanor in confronting ferocious wolves is to behave like doves, as Jesus did when viciously attacked (1 Peter 2:21–23). The gentleness and guiltlessness (innocence) of a dove are proverbial.[171] Watson says, "We must have the innocence of the dove, that we may not betray the truth; and the wisdom of the serpent, that we may not betray ourselves."[172] Believers are to be irreproachable and godly, so as to honor Christ and have firm footing in standing for the truth. D. A. Carson comments, "So Jesus' disciples, in their mission as sheep among wolves, must be 'shrewd,' avoiding conflicts and attacks where possible; but they must also be 'innocent,' i.e., not so cautious, suspicious and cunning that circumspection degenerates into fear or elusiveness."[173] S. K. Weber says, "Grace must govern our compassion toward others, as well as our own example of integrity through all circumstances. But grace and truth are not mutually exclusive. They are the two sides of one eternal coin. Truth must govern our perceptions of danger and the faults of others."[174] See Chapter 15, *Civility toward Persecutors*.

The Christian is not to be anxious or afraid in the time of trials. Unflinching trust in God that He stands with us in the furnace grants peace and courage to endure. "If God be for us, who can be against us?" (Romans 8:31). Jesus said, "And fear not them which kill the body, but are not able to kill the soul; but rather fear Him which is able to destroy both soul and body in hell" (Matthew 10:28). Albert Barnes comments "that is, people, who have no power to injure the soul, the immortal part. The body is a small matter in comparison with the soul. Temporal death is a slight thing compared with eternal death. He directs them, therefore, not to be alarmed at the prospect of temporal death, but to fear God, who can destroy both soul and body forever. This passage proves that the bodies of the wicked will be raised up to be punished forever."[175]

At the howl of the wolf, the sheep looks to their shepherd for protection. He that "sends" also "defends." He that sent you into an unfriendly, hostile world to proclaim the Gospel (Matthew 10:6–7) is He that prizes you (1 Peter 2:9–10), protects you (Psalm 18:2–4), provides for you (Matthew 10:9–10) and will preserve you (Psalm 23:4). He triumphantly faced the wolves when upon the same mission (John 16:33). And in and through Him, every believer is enabled and empowered to do the same (Revelation 12:11). Matthew Henry remarks, "They are as sheep among wolves; that is frightful. But Christ sends them forth; that is comfortable, for he that sends them forth will protect them and bear them out."[176] I. D. Campbell says the saints "will not be left without help. On the one hand, the Holy Spirit will help them; on the other, they are to remember that they are walking in Christ's footsteps (Matthew 10:24–25)."[177]

Opposition is the door to opportunity to testify of Christ.

The saint's persecution is purposed to give occasion for a witness. Jesus said, "On my account you will be brought before governors and kings as *witnesses* to them and to the Gentiles" (Matthew 10:18 NIV). Opposition is the door to opportunity to testify of Christ. In Sudan, Michael was placed in prison for the preaching of the Gospel. The jail was so crowded that prisoners had to sleep in shifts. However, instead of complaining about the experience, Michael said, "It was a perfect evangelism opportunity."[178]

14
Dykes of Courage

"Do not fear the face of man. Remember how small their anger will appear in eternity."[179]

~ Robert Murray M'Cheyne

"More glorious is the soldier," states Tertullian, "pierced with a javelin in battle, than he who has a safe skin as a fugitive [a believer that out of cowardice flees persecution]."[180] Oh, for a courage like that of William Lithgow, tortured during the Spanish Inquisition, who said, "I fear neither death nor fire. I am prepared for both, so do your worst!"[181]

As Jesus approached the cross and death accompanied by the disciples (heroes of the faith), the Bible says, "as they (disciples) followed, they were afraid" (Mark 10:32). To the disciples' credit, fear of the unknown (what persecution may lay ahead) did not stagger their faith in Christ, weaken their allegiance to Christ, nor impede their mission for Christ. Despite being afraid, they remained confident and courageous. Mark Twain said, "Courage is resistance to fear, mastery of fear, not absence of fear."[182] Courage in the midst of fear must be exhibited by all believers in times of persecution or execution. Paul says, "For God hath not given us the spirit of fear; but of power, and of love, and of a sound mind" (II Timothy 1:7). Martin Luther King, Jr., said, "We must constantly build dykes of courage to hold back the flood of fear."[183]

From whence is courage instilled (dykes of courage erected) in the heart? The dyke of a **righteous life.** "The righteous are bold as a lion" (Proverbs 28:1). Gregory said, "The lion is not afraid in the onset of beasts, because he knows well that he is stronger than them all. Whence the fearlessness of a righteous man is rightly compared to a lion, because, when he beholds any rising against him, he returns to the confidence of his mind and knows that he overcomes all his adversaries because he loves Him alone whom he cannot in any way lose against his will."[184] An African proverb says, "The lion does not turn around when a small dog barks."

The dyke of **trust in the Lord.** "Be of good courage, and he shall strengthen your heart, all ye that hope in the LORD" (Psalm 31:24). A. W. Pink states, "Faith is a grace which draws down from Heaven whatever blessing of God is most needful to the saint, and therefore does it stand him in as good stead in the night of adversity as in the day of prosperity. Faith imparts a steadfastness of purpose, a noble courage, a tranquility of mind, which no human education or fleshly effort can supply. Faith makes the righteous as bold as a lion, refusing to recant though horrible tortures and a martyr's death be the only alternatives."[185]

> I saw the martyr at the stake;
> The flames could not his courage shake
>   Nor death his soul appall.
> I asked him whence his strength was giv'n;
> He looked triumphantly to Heav'n
>   And answered, "Christ is all."

> ~ Anonymous

The dyke of the **infilling of the Holy Spirit.** "They were all filled with the Holy Ghost, and they spake the word of God with boldness" (Acts 4:31). When the Holy Spirit is not simply resident, but president in the believer, a holy boldness is manifested (Ephesians 5:18).

The dyke of **God's promises.** "The LORD has kept all the good promises" (1 Kings 8:56 NCV). Rest upon the divine promise of Joshua 1:9 in times of affliction: "Be strong and of a good courage; be not afraid, neither be thou dismayed: for the Lord thy God is with thee whithersoever thou goest."

The dyke of an **awareness that God is greater than our foe.** "Greater is He that is in you, than he that is in the world" (1 John 4:4).

The dyke of **stillness before God.** "Wait on the LORD…and he shall strengthen thine heart: wait, I say, on the LORD" (Psalm 27:14).

The dyke of **emboldening by the emboldened.** Believers shore up the courage of each other in the trials of life in three ways. *Companionship.* Jonathan strengthened David's grip on God at a time when he was afraid (1 Samuel 23:15–17).

Example. Billy Graham said, "Courage is contagious. When a brave man takes a stand, the spines of others are often stiffened."[186] An historical story substantiates Graham's point. At the beginning of the twentieth century, Christians taking the Gospel to China met violent resistance from Chinese rebels (Boxer Rebellion). A mission school for students studying for the ministry was attacked. The rebels offered freedom to every student who would trample over a cross laid at the school's only unblocked exit; the others would be shot. The first six students trampled upon the cross to their freedom. The seventh student, a teenage girl, walked up to the cross, knelt down by it, and then walked around it and was killed. The remaining ninety-two students, infused by her faith and courage, did the same. Oh, the power of a righteous and courageous life to incite others to stand their ground for Christ regardless of cost or consequence.

Prayer. Ask God, on behalf of others and yourself, for increased boldness and strength to stand unflinchingly in the hour of persecution. Jesus prayed for Peter that his "faith fail not" (Luke 22:32) in the hour of trial. What a glorious thought, to know that in persecution Jesus is interceding the same for us!

The dyke of the **ministry of angels.** Angels are "ministering spirits" to the redeemed (Hebrews 1:14). The Greek word for *minister* refers to "serviceable labor and assistance."[187] "They are ministering spirits, or heavenly assistants, who are continually active today in building the body of Christ—advancing the ministry of Jesus and the building of His church."[188]

Two Scripture texts indicate the *saint* (not unbeliever) in fact has a guardian angel that overwatches him. In Matthew 18:10, Jesus states that children have "their angels" that are on standby to care for them at the Lord's command. The second text is Acts 12, where an angel freed Peter from prison. Afterward, Peter knocked on the door of a house where a prayer meeting was ongoing for his release.

In discovering it was Peter, the servant, due to being overcome with excitement, unthinkingly left him outside while she ran to tell the others the good news. The praying saints, however, counted the person at the door as Peter's angel.

Angels excel in strength to assist the saint. The psalmist says, "Bless the LORD, ye his angels, that excel in strength, that do his commandments, hearkening unto the voice of his word" (Psalm 103:20), and, "Praise the Lord, all you warriors [angels] of his, you servants [angels] of his who carry out his desires" (Psalm 103:21 NET). Their great power and strength ("excel in strength") safeguard the saint against the wiles of the Devil, adversaries and mishaps. The psalmist declared, "For he will order his angels to protect you wherever you go" (Psalm 91:11 NLT). C. H. Spurgeon states, "If our eyes could be opened, we should see horses of fire and chariots of fire about the servants of the Lord; for we have come to an innumerable company of angels, who are all watchers and protectors of the seed royal."[189] Angels are dispatched by God especially in times of emergency to warn, help and/or protect the saints (Daniel 6:22). "Much of their work is to oppose the malice of evil spirits, who seek our hurt, and to defend us from their rage and subtlety (deceptiveness; skill to be unnoticeable)."[190] Angels provide comfort, guidance and provision for saints experiencing suffering and persecution for the sake of Christ. See Daniel 10:19.

Billy Graham shares an interesting story in the book *Angels, God's Secret Agents*. "The Reverend John G. Paton, a missionary in the New Hebrides Islands, tells a thrilling story involving the protective care of angels. Hostile natives surrounded his mission headquarters one night, intent on burning the Paton's out and killing them. John Paton and his wife prayed all during that terror-filled night that God would deliver them. When daylight came, they were amazed to see the attackers unaccountably leave. They thanked God for delivering them. A year later, the chief of the tribe was converted to Jesus Christ, and Mr. Paton, remembering what had happened, asked the chief what had kept him and his men from burning down the house and killing them. The chief replied in surprise, 'Who were all those men you had with you there?' The missionary answered, 'There were no men there, just my wife and I.' The chief argued that they had seen many men standing guard—hundreds of big men in shining garments with drawn swords in their hands. They seemed to circle the mission station so that the natives were afraid to attack. Only then did Mr. Paton realize that God had sent His angels to protect them. The chief agreed that there was no other explanation. Could it be that God had sent a legion of angels to protect His servants whose lives were being endangered?"[191] See a similar incident recorded in 2 Kings 6:14–17. Graham testifies that at moments of special need, he was attended to by angels.[192]

Ministering angels dispatched by God for our assistance in warfare are often unnoticed (Hebrews 13:2). Knowledge of their presence has to increase the believer's boldness in facing oppression.

Socrates remarks, "He is a man of courage who does not run away but remains at his post and fights against the enemy."[193] Face persecution boldly. On campus or athletic field, in the political arena or workplace, light a candle for Christ that no man can extinguish. Don't cower down. Never be ashamed of Christ. Take the ribbing and rejection. Never recant beliefs and biblical convictions, regardless of cost or consequence. Dietrich Bonhoeffer, German pastor, hanged on April 9, 1945, for participating in a plot to kill Hitler, said "They [messengers of the Gospel] must not fear men. Men can do them no harm, for the power of men ceases with the death of the body. But they overcome the fear of death with the fear of God. Those who are still afraid of men have no fear of God, and those who have fear of God have ceased to be afraid of men. All preachers of the Gospel will do well to recollect this saying daily."[194]

> Fear not the foe, thou flock of God;
> Fear not the sword, the spear, the rod;
>> Fear not the foe!
> He fights in vain who fights with thee;
> Soon shalt thou see his armies flee,
>> Himself laid low.

Come, cheer thee to the toil and fight;
'Tis God, thy God, defends the right;
   He leads thee on.
His sword shall scatter every foe;
His shield shall ward off every blow;
   The crown is won.

His is the battle, His the power;
His is the triumph in that hour;
   In Him be strong.
So round thy brow the wreath shall twine,
So shall the victory be thine
   And thine the song.

Not long the sigh, the toil, the sweat;
Not long the fight-day's wasting heat;
   The shadows come.
Slack not thy weapon in the fight;
Courage! for God defends the right;
   Strike home! Strike home!

                     ~ Horatius Bonar (1861)

Found among the papers of a young African pastor in Zimbabwe after he was martyred was this brazen statement: "I'm a part of the fellowship of the unashamed. The dye has been cast. I have stepped over the line. The decision has been made. I'm a disciple of His, and I won't look back, let up, slow down, back away, or be still. My past is redeemed. My present makes sense. My future is secure. I'm finished with low living, sight walking, small planning, smooth knees, colorless dreams, tamed visions, mundane talking, cheap living, and dwarfed goals. I no longer need preeminence, prosperity, position, promotions, plaudits, or popularity. I don't have to be right or first or tops or recognized or praised or rewarded. I live by faith, lean on His presence, walk by patience, lift by prayer, and labor by the Holy Spirit's power. My face is set. My gait is fast. My goal is Heaven. My road may be narrow, my way rough, my companions few; but my Guide is reliable, and my mission is clear. I will not be bought, compromised, detoured, lured away, turned back, deluded, or delayed. I will not flinch in the face of sacrifice or hesitate in the presence of the adversary. I will not negotiate at the table of the enemy, ponder at the pool of popularity, or meander in the maze of mediocrity. I won't give up, shut up, or let up, until I have stayed up, stored up, prayed up, paid up, and preached up for the cause of Christ. I am a disciple of Jesus. I must give until I drop, preach until all know, and work until He comes. And when He does come for His own, He'll have no problems recognizing me. My colors will be clear!"[195] See Romans 1:16.

A. W. Tozer pointedly said, "The true follower of Christ will not ask, 'If I embrace this truth, what will it cost me?' Rather, he will say, 'This is truth. God help me walk in it, let come what may!'"[196]

15
Civility Toward Persecutors

"Christian men are not at war with any man that walks the earth. We are at war with infidelity, but the persons of infidels we love and pray for; we are at warfare with any heresy, but we have no enmity against heretics; we are opposed to and cry war to the knife with everything that opposes God and his truth, but towards every man we would still endeavor to carry out the holy maxim, 'Love your enemies, do good to them that hate you.'"[197]

~ C. H. Spurgeon

The Christian's response to persecution is, "Bless them which persecute you" (Romans 12:14).

Bless them that curse you. Albert Barnes says, "Bless only; or continue to bless, however long or aggravated may be the injury. Do not be provoked to anger, or to cursing, by any injury, persecution, or reviling. This is one of the most severe and difficult duties of the Christian religion, and it is a duty which nothing else but religion will enable people to perform."[198] The response seems absurd and unreasonable. But Jesus underscores how imperative it is, saying, "Love your enemies, do good to those who hate you, bless those who curse you, pray for those who abuse you" (Luke 6:27–28 ESV). That is, instead of reciprocating hatred for hatred, demonstrate acts of loving-kindness to the persecutor. Spurgeon comments, "For cruel words return warmer love and increased kindness. The most renowned weapon for a Christian to fight his antagonists with is that of overcoming evil with good. Evil to evil is beastlike, and no Christian will indulge in it; but good for evil is Christlike, and we must practice it. This is the surest way to victory. Yield everything but what it would be wrong to yield. Never grow angry. Keep cool, and let the railing be all on one side."[199]

Pray for those that hurt you. "Pray for those who mistreat [abuse] you" (Luke 6:28 CEB). John Gill says, "What Christ here commands and advises to, He himself did; for as He hung upon the cross, He prayed for His crucifiers, who were then using Him in the most despiteful, as well as cruel, manner, saying, "Father, forgive them; for they know not what they do"; and in this He has left us an example, that we should tread in His steps."[200] Pray that your persecutor(s) will experience a supernatural heart and attitude change—much like the transformation of Paul, the severe persecutor of the early church (Acts 9:1–19). Justin Martyr said, "We pray for our enemies; we seek to persuade those who hate us without cause to live conformably to the goodly precepts of Christ, that they may become partakers with us of the joyful hope of blessings from God, the Lord of all."[201]

Return good to them that are your enemies. The Bible says, "If thine *enemy* be hungry, give him bread to eat; and if he be thirsty, give him water to drink: For thou shalt *heap coals of fire* upon his head, and the LORD shall reward thee" (Proverbs 25:21–22). The Christian's response to one who is an "enemy" (literally, "one who hates you") is not to get even or do the person harm but to exhibit love and kindness toward him while praying for his conversion and good. Our Lord instructs, "Love your enemies, bless them that curse you, do good to them that hate you, and *pray for them* which despitefully use you, and persecute [mistreat, hurt] you" (Matthew 5:44). In such display of kindness, the Christian is 'heaping coals of fire upon his head' (Proverbs 25:22). John MacArthur comments, "As metals are melted by placing fiery coals on them, so is the heart of an enemy softened by such kindness."[202]

"The sinner is benefited by the clemency shown to him, that the requital of evil by good brings the offender to a better mind and aids his spiritual life. The unmerited kindness which he receives forces upon him the consciousness of his ill doing, which is accompanied by the sharp pain of regret [heaping of hot coals upon his head]."[203] Saith Matthew Henry, "The way to turn an enemy into a friend is to act towards him in a friendly manner. If it does not gain him, it will aggravate his sin and punishment [heap hot coals upon his head]. Whether he relent towards thee or not, the Lord shall reward thee."[204] Exhibiting the exact opposite of what an enemy expects (with the right motive) may be the means of his repentance and conversion. Jesus Christ certainly acted accordingly toward us, for "while we were yet sinners, Christ died for us" (Romans 5:8).

Turn the other cheek to him that smites you (Matthew 5:39). Oswald Chambers says, "Naturally, if a man does not hit back, it is because he is a coward; but spiritually, if a man does not hit back, it is a manifestation of the Son of God in him. When you are insulted, you must not only not resent it, but make it an occasion to exhibit the Son of God. You cannot imitate the disposition of Jesus; it is either there or it is not. To the saint, personal insult becomes the occasion of revealing the incredible sweetness of the Lord Jesus."[205] With this Dietrich Bonhoeffer agrees stating, "The Christian must treat his enemy as a brother and requite his hostility with love. His behavior must be determined not by the way others treat him, but by the treatment he himself receives from Jesus; it has only one source, and that is the will of Jesus."[206]

Forgive them that mistreat you (Matthew 5:44). Stephen, when being stoned, asked for the forgiveness of them that hurled the stones upon him (Acts 7:60). Don't allow your hurts to turn into hates. Whether or not someone deserves forgiveness is not the issue. Kent Crockett states, "We base our forgiveness on what God has done for us, not on what another person has done to us."[207] Forgiveness ought to be granted not because someone deserves it but because God out of His infinite love forgave us and asks that we do the same unto our persecutors. "And be ye kind one to another, tenderhearted, forgiving one another, even as God for Christ's sake hath forgiven you" (Ephesians 4:32). An imprisoned Christian testified, "The days became longer and the nights longer" amidst the guards' relentless and cruel torture. Hate for the guards that inflicted the pain intensified. And then the man realized that the hatred was multiplying the torment. As he put it, "I was being tormented physically without, but also spiritually within by the hate." Upon praying for God to grant supernatural ability to replace the hate with His love, peace flooded his soul, and his torture was turned into a blessing to the torturers.[208] He did what Jonathan Edwards said

Christians will do in times of inflamed hatred for one's persecutors; he allowed it to chase him "into the arms of Jesus, his best Friend, with the more delight."[209]

Corrie Ten Boom rightly states, "Forgiveness is an act of the will, and the will can function regardless of the temperature of the heart."[210] "Forgiveness," states Jon Courson, "doesn't have to do with feelings. Forgiveness is a decision we make. If we decide to forgive, feelings will follow in due season."[211] John MacArthur said, "Forgiveness is first of all an act of the will. It is not hypocrisy to will forgiveness when the emotions are screaming for vengeance. Be obedient to the Lord regardless of how you feel."[212] Shove past the emotions of hurt, and with the mind determine to forgive them that mistreat you.

Albert Barnes summarizes the text (Matthew 5:11) beautifully: "When thus reviled or persecuted, we are to be meek, patient, humble; not angry; not reviling again, but endeavoring to do good to our persecutors and slanderers (2 Timothy 2:24–25). In this way many have been convinced of the power and excellence of that religion which they were persecuting and reviling. They have seen that nothing else but Christianity could impart such patience and meekness to the persecuted and have, by this means, been constrained to submit themselves to the Gospel of Jesus. Long since it became a proverb that "the blood of the martyrs is the seed of the church."[213] Barnes continues, "Each one who is oppressed and wronged, therefore, has an eminent opportunity to show a spirit which will honor the Gospel; and the martyr may do more to honor the Gospel than if he were both permitted to enjoy liberty and life undisturbed."[214]

16
Comfort in the Furnace

"There is a God in Heaven who overrules all things for the best, and this is the comfort of my soul."[215]

~ David Brainerd

Numerous sources of consolation for the hour of peril are graciously provided by our Lord.

Be comforted in knowing that suffering is great gain. "Did any Christian," asks Spurgeon, "ever suffer yet by persecution—really suffer by it? Does he ever really lose by it? No; it is quite the reverse. We gain by it."[216] What does the persecuted one gain? Divine moldability, spiritual maturity, purifying sanctification, growth in prayer and meditation, platform for evangelism, affirmation of faith, and the commendation of Christ. Hyatt states, "That which the Devil effects in malice, with a view to their (the believers') ruin, the Savior permits in mercy, with a view to their advantage. The faith and the patience of suffering saints confound Satan, encourage the Church, and glorify Christ."[217] This Paul understood, and bore testimony: "For to me to live is Christ, and to die is gain. But what things were gain to me, those I counted loss for Christ. Yea doubtless, and I count all things but loss for the excellency of the knowledge of Christ Jesus my Lord: for whom I have suffered the loss of all things, and do count them but dung, that I may win Christ" (Philippians 1:21 and 3:7–8).

Be comforted in the assurance of Christ's constant companionship. Christ is He that said, "I will never leave thee, nor forsake thee" (Hebrews 13:5). He is the Fourth Man in the fire (Daniel 3:25). He is our refuge and strength, a very present help in trouble (Psalm 46:1). He is that Friend that sticketh closer than a brother (Proverbs 18:24). He is the God of *all* comfort (2 Corinthians 1:3–4). He is the Lord that heals thee (Exodus 15:26). He is the God that binds up all our wounds (Psalm 147:3). Spurgeon says, "Remember, too, that if you have extraordinary troubles, *Jesus will be doubly near to you.*

This is the greatest comfort of all, for in all your afflictions, He is afflicted. The old covenantors said they never worshipped God with so much joy as in the glens and among the hills when Claverhouse's dragoons were after them. His bosom is very soft and warm for those who are rejected of all men for His sake. He has a marvelous way of unveiling His face to those whose faces are covered with shame because of their love to Him."[218] "No man ever suffers persecution alone," states Barclay; "if a man is called upon to bear material loss, the failure of friends, slander, loneliness, even the death of love, for his principles, he will not be left alone. Christ will be nearer to him than at any other time."[219] See Daniel 3:19–25. "It is well to bear trial if 'God' be our Friend."[220]

> Oh, while Thou dost smile upon me,
>   God of wisdom, love, and might,
> Foes may hate and friends may shun me;
>   Show thy face, and all is bright.
>
> Man may trouble and distress me;
>   'Twill but drive me to thy breast.
> Life with trials hard may press me;
>   Heav'n will bring me sweeter rest.
>
> Oh, 'tis not in grief to harm me
>   While thy love is left to me;
> Oh, 'twere not in joy to charm me
>   Were that joy unmixed with Thee.
>
> ~ Henry Francis Lyte (1825)

"How blessed to be in fellowship," writes H. A. Ironside, "with the Father, the Son, and the Holy Spirit, so that one can enter into and enjoy the comfort They delight to give! What greater privilege can we have on earth than to enjoy the abiding presence of the GOD of all comfort as we face the perplexities and bitter disappointments that we are called upon to endure?"[221] See John 14:16, 26; 15:26; 16:7. It is foolish to have such comfort readily available and yet left untapped as was the case with the disciples in Mark 10. 'They followed Him in fear' (Mark 10:32). Like Rachel, they "refused to be comforted" (Jeremiah 31:15). See Deuteronomy 31:6 and Isaiah 42:3.

Be comforted in the fact that persecutors are under God's divine authority and rule. Spurgeon states, "You may have this for your comfort, that the persecutor is in God's hands. He cannot do more than God lets him, and if God permits him to annoy, you may cheerfully bear it."[222] Robert Murray M'Cheyne said, "Are we not all immortal till our work is done?"

Be comforted in the fact that martyrdom is a conquest of Satan. Barclay says, "The martyr has proved superior to every seduction and to every threat and even to the violence of Satan. Here is a dramatic truth for life—every time we choose to suffer rather than to be disloyal is the defeat of Satan. The victory of the martyrs is won through the blood of the Lamb."[223]

Be comforted in the fact that the enemies of God will be held accountable for their infliction of pain to the saint. The Bible says, "All who rage against you will surely be ashamed and disgraced; those who oppose you will be as nothing and perish....For I am the Lord your God who takes hold of your right hand and says to you, Do not fear; I will help you" (Isaiah 41:11, 13 NIV). Spurgeon continues, "The best day that ever dawns on a sinner brings a curse with it. Sinners may have many feast days, but no safe days."[224] A payday awaits all who harm God's children for biblical beliefs and righteous endeavors. The saints ultimately will be publicly vindicated (Matthew 10:26). R. G. Lee in the renowned sermon *Payday, Someday* says, "'Payday—Someday' is written in the constitution of God's universe. The retributive providence of God is a reality as certainly as the laws of gravitation are a reality....Even though the mill of God grinds slowly, it grinds to powder. Yes, the judgments of God often have leaden heels and travel slowly. But they always have iron hands and crush completely."[225]

Be comforted in the fact that it's God's fight, not ours. "But if it be of God, ye cannot overthrow it; lest haply ye be found even *to fight against God*" (Acts 5:39). Barnes says, "The word *fight* occurs nowhere else in the New Testament. To fight against God is to oppose Him or to maintain an attitude of hostility against Him. It is an attitude that is most fearful in its character and will most certainly be attended with an overthrow. No condition can be more awful than such an opposition to the Almighty, no overthrow more terrible than what must follow such opposition. Compare Acts 9:5; Acts 23:9. Opposition to the "gospel" in the Scriptures is uniformly regarded as opposition to God (Matthew 12:30; Luke 11:23)."[226]

All who endeavor to silence the church; restrain religious observances, practices and worship; oppose the doctrines of God; seek the abolition of religious liberties; manifest disdain for Christ and His followers; and instigate and inflict torment on believers with whom they disagree theologically and politically will have to contend (the strongest and mightiest opposition) with Almighty God. "The LORD himself will fight for you. Just stay calm" (Exodus 14:14 NLT). "The battle belongs to the LORD, and he will help us defeat all of you" (I Samuel 17:47 ERV). "Infidels and scoffers will gain nothing by opposing God. They have thus far been thwarted, and unsuccessful (for over 2,000 years); and they will be still."[227] Therefore, be ye comforted and calmed in the face of persecution. See Romans 8:37.

Be comforted through the promises of God. Calm, courage and comfort are dispensed from the Scriptures. Albert Barnes says, "With the promises of the Bible in our hand, we may hail persecutions and thank God that, amid so many sorrows, He has furnished such abundant consolations."[228] See 2 Peter 1:4. Martin Luther wrote, "It is much easier to learn than to believe that we who have by us the Word of God and receive it are surrounded with divine aid. If we were surrounded by walls of steel and fire, we should feel secure and defy the Devil. But the property of faith is not to be proud of what the eye sees, but to rely on what the Word reveals."[229]

Be comforted through the fraternity of like-minded believers. "He comforts us when we are in trouble, so that we can share that same comfort with others in trouble" (2 Corinthians 1:4 CEV). Paul sent Timothy to uplift the Thessalonian saints in their time of great affliction. In I Thessalonians he writes, "We sent him to strengthen you, to encourage you in your faith, and to keep you from being shaken by the troubles you were going through. But you know that we are destined for such troubles" (I Thessalonians 3:2-3 NLT). It was Jonathan that strengthened David's spiritual grip and encouraged him when he was persecuted by King Saul (1 Samuel 23:16). Comfort provided by the household of faith strengthens the Christian in crisis.

> Comfort confirms the Christian in crisis.

Be comforted in the fact that suffering for Christ is a great gift. Paul wrote, "For unto you it is given in the behalf of Christ, not only to believe on him, but also to suffer for his sake" (Philippians 1:29). It is a privilege both to "believe in Christ" and to "suffer" for Him. To believe in Christ is a privilege, for it is in and through Him that our sins are forgiven and we are reconciled to God (1 John 2:2 and Colossians 1:20). John Piper said, "It's granted to you. It's given to you. It's a gift to you with a big bow, that you will suffer."[230] Matthew Henry says, "If we suffer reproach and loss for Christ, we are to reckon it a great gift, and prize it accordingly, always provided we behave under our sufferings with the genuine temper of martyrs and confessors."[231]

Be comforted through exhibiting a strong resistance to the intimidation and harassment of Satan. "Neither give place to the devil" (Ephesians 4:27). Do not yield to the hostile criticism, sarcasm, and evil accusations induced and inflamed by Satan to discourage and dishearten. Instead, send them back to where they originated, to Satan, saying "Refused." A. W. Tozer said, "I'm not afraid of the Devil. The Devil can handle me—he's got judo I never heard of. But he can't handle the One to whom I'm joined; he can't handle the One to whom I'm united; he can't handle the One whose nature dwells in my nature."[232] See 1 John 4:4.

Be comforted by maintaining a clear conscience. A conscience void of guilt is a great joy. To do what is right, for the proper reason, at the right time, and in the correct manner grants inward peace despite hostile forces pounding the soul and body from without. To injure the conscience is to lose that consolation and happiness. [233]

Be comforted in the fact that present suffering is preparation for greater glory in Heaven. Paul says, "Therefore we do not lose heart. Even though our outward man is perishing, yet the inward man is being renewed day by day. For our light affliction, which is but for a moment, is working for us a far more exceeding and eternal weight of glory" (2 Corinthians 4:16–17 NKJV). A man whose grief was beyond measure due to the death of his wife, loss of his job, exhausted savings, and forfeiture of his home was near the breaking point. The only thing positive going for him was his faith, and it was growing weaker. One day he noticed men doing stonework on a church—one of them was chiseling a triangular piece of rock. Scouring the building in vain to see where it might fit, he asked, "Where are you going to put that?" The stonemason pointed toward the top of the building and said, "See that little opening up near the spire? That's where it goes. I'm shaping it down here so it will fit in up there." Tears filled the man's eyes as he pondered the words – "Shaping it down here so it will fit in up there." God used that experience to reassure him that all his pain would be for eternal gain, that He was chiseling away at his life to prepare him for his "fit up there." Nothing experienced is wasted, not our tears of sorrow, anguish of soul, stress and anxiety, losses, suffering, and pain. God promises to use them all for our future gain in Heaven. Hallelujah.

Be comforted in the fact that the gates of Hell will not prevail against the church or Christ's followers. "And I say also unto thee, that thou art Peter, and upon this rock I will build my church; and the gates of hell shall not prevail against it" (Matthew 16:18). Adam Clarke explains, "In ancient times the gates of fortified cities were used to hold councils in and were usually places of great strength. Our Lord's expression means that neither the plots, stratagems, nor strength of Satan and his angels should ever so far prevail as to destroy the sacred truths in the above confession [the 'rock' is Peter's confession that Jesus is the Messiah who came to save the lost]. Sometimes the gates are taken for the troops which issue out from them. We may firmly believe that though Hell should open her gates and vomit out her Devil and all his angels to fight against Christ and His saints, ruin and discomfiture must be the consequence on their part; as the arm of the Omnipotent must prevail."[234]

Be comforted in knowing that though martyrdom kills the body, it doth not destroy the soul (Romans 8:35). A variant interpretation (to that previously shared) of Matthew 16:18 says that "the gates of hell" refer to the gates of death. That is, death itself will not have power over the saint to experience the resurrection from the dead and eternity in Heaven. "O death, where is thy sting? O grave, where is thy victory?" (1 Corinthians 15:55). "Through the grave and gate of death they shall pass to a joyful resurrection."[235] Both interpretations are applicable; neither the power of death nor the powers of Satan and his cohorts shall prevail against Christ's church, cause and people. What wondrous comfort it is to possess such glorious promises, especially in the hour of oppression for the faith.

Commenting on Revelation 6:9 (martyrs in Heaven), Albert Barnes states, "This is one of the incidental proofs in the Bible that the soul does not cease to exist at death and also that it does not cease to be conscious or does not sleep until the resurrection. These souls of the martyrs are represented as still in existence, as remembering what had occurred on the earth, as interested in what was now taking place, as engaged in prayer, and as manifesting earnest desires for the divine interposition to avenge the wrongs which they had suffered."[236] See John 12:25.

Be comforted in the fact that the Holy Spirit will enable your defense. Jesus said, "But when they arrest you, do not worry about what to say or how to say it. At that time you will be given what to say, For it will not be you speaking, but the Spirit of your Father speaking through you" (Matthew 10:19–20 NIV). The admonition is repeated in Luke's Gospel: "Settle it therefore in your hearts, not to meditate before what ye shall answer: For I will give you a mouth and wisdom, which all your adversaries shall not be able to gainsay nor resist" (Luke 21:14–15). William MacDonald states, "They need not rehearse what they would say when on trial. When the time came, the Spirit of God would give them divine wisdom to answer in such a way as to glorify Christ and utterly confuse and frustrate their accusers."[237] How consoling and reassuring it is to know that when brought before rulers and judges for Christ's sake, the Holy Spirit will give us utterance (dictate what is to be said). This fact is amazingly borne out in Peter and John when before the council (Acts 4:1–13) and in Stephen's defense before the Sanhedrin (Acts 7:2–54).

Be comforted in the fact that Christ soon will return for His children. Billy Graham said, "No Christian has the right to go around wringing his hands, wondering what we are to do in the face of the present world situation. The Scripture says that in the midst of persecution, confusion, wars, and rumors of wars, we are to comfort one another with the knowledge that Jesus Christ is coming back in triumph, glory, and majesty."[238] See Titus 2:13. The persecuted saints in the first century found hope and encouragement in their affliction in the use of two passwords (to identify foe from friend). One of the passwords was "till He come" and the second was "maranatha" or "Lord, come!"[239] The eschatological passwords (and meanings) uplifted the distraught saints. Richard Sibbs said, "The life of a Christian is wondrously ruled in this world by the consideration and meditation of the life of another world."[240]

Be comforted in the fact of Heaven. "For ye had compassion of me in my bonds, and took joyfully the spoiling of your goods, knowing in yourselves that ye have in heaven a better and an enduring substance" (Hebrews 10:34). Consolation and joy in suffering is possible by knowing with all certainty that things far better than any earthly substance await in Heaven and that these are permanent, unlike the best things of this life. See John 14:1–3 and Revelation 21:4–5. Saith Henry Ward Beecher, "Living is death; dying is life. On this side of the grave, we are exiles; on that, citizens; on this side, orphans; on that, children; on this side, captives; on that, freemen; on this side, disguised, unknown; on that, disclosed and proclaimed as the sons of God."[241]

Hasten on from grace to glory,
    Armed by faith and winged by prayer.
Heav'n's eternal day's before thee;
    God's own hand shall guide thee there.

Soon shall close thy earthly mission;
    Swift shall pass thy pilgrim days,
Hope soon change to glad fruition,
    Faith to sight, and prayer to praise.

~ Henry Francis Lyte (1825)

Be comforted in persecution in the fact that it's not your cross, but Christ's cross that you bear. Spurgeon writes, "When you are molested for your piety, when your religion brings the trial of cruel mockings upon you, then remember it is not your cross; it is Christ's cross. And how delightful is it to carry the cross of our Lord Jesus! You carry the cross after Him. You have blessed company; your path is marked with the footprints of your Lord. The mark of his blood-red shoulder is upon that heavy burden. 'Tis His cross, and He goes before you as a shepherd goes before his sheep. Take up your cross daily and follow Him."[242]

Be comforted in persecution in the fact it serves to fashion you more into the likeness of Christ. "Unaccountable, this!" said the Wax, as from the flame it dropped, melting upon the Paper beneath.

"Do not grieve," said the Paper; "I am sure it is all right."

"I was never in such agony!" exclaimed the Wax, still dropping.

"It is not without a good design and will end well," replied the Paper.

The Wax was unable to reply at once, owing to a strong pressure; and when it again looked up it bore a beautiful impression, the counterpart of the seal which had been applied to it. "Ah! I comprehend now," said the Wax, no longer in suffering. "I was softened in order to receive this lovely durable impress. Yes; I see now it was all right, because it has given to me the beautiful likeness which I could not otherwise have obtained."[243]

See 2 Corinthians 4:8–10 and Romans 5:3–4.

Though lengthy, the words of Samuel Rutherford are powerfully impactful. He writes, "If your Lord calls you to suffering, do not be dismayed, for He will provide a deeper portion of Christ in your suffering. The softest pillow will be placed under your head though you must set your bare feet among thorns. Do not be afraid at suffering for Christ, for He has a sweet peace for a sufferer. God has called you to Christ's side, and if the wind is now in His face, you cannot expect to rest on the sheltered side of the hill. You cannot be above your Master who received many an innocent stroke. The greatest temptation out of Hell is to live without trials. A pool of standing water will turn stagnant. Faith grows more with the sharp winter storm in its face. Grace withers without adversity. You cannot sneak quietly into Heaven without a cross. Crosses form us into His image. They cut away the pieces of our corruption. Lord, cut, carve, wound; Lord, do anything to perfect Your image in us and make us fit for glory! We need winnowing before we enter the kingdom of God. Oh, what I owe to the file, hammer, and furnace! Why should I be surprised at the plough that makes such deep furrows in my soul? Whatever direction the wind blows, it will blow us to the Lord. His hand will direct us safely to the heavenly shore to find the weight of eternal glory. As we look back to our pains and suffering, we shall see that suffering is not worthy to be compared to our first night's welcome home in Heaven. If we could smell of Heaven and our country above, our crosses would not bite us. Lay all your loads by faith on Christ, ease yourself, and let Him bear all. He can, He does, and He will bear you. Whether God comes with a rod or a crown, He comes with Himself. "Have courage, I am your salvation!" Welcome, welcome Jesus!"[244]

17
Combative Faith

"It is impossible to be a true soldier of Jesus Christ and not fight."[245]

~ *John Gresham Machen*

Jude says every believer "should earnestly contend for the faith which was once delivered unto the saints" (Jude 3). Note the traits of the Christian's defensible faith.

It is a common faith, available and sufficient to redeem from sin and its penalty, regardless of face, race or place (Jude 3a). It is a common faith, for it has a common source (Christ Jesus), provides what *all* sinners need (reconciliation to God) and is the same that all who are "born-gain" enjoy. Its benefits (peace, pardon, pleasure, preservation and Heaven) are inexhaustible, limitless and free. Alexander Maclaren said, "If it is true that salvation is a gift from God, then it is quite plain that the only thing that we require is an outstretched hand. It is no arbitrary appointment. The only possible way of possessing 'the common salvation' is by the exercise of 'the common faith.'"[246]

It is a complete faith; nothing more needs to be added or can be added (Jude 3b). It entails Christ's incarnation, sinless life, substitutionary death, resurrection and ascension, and promise to return for His church. It declares the essential doctrines of the Christian faith, including the depravity of man (sin); divinity and redemptive work of Christ Jesus; salvation by grace through faith in Christ alone; work of the Holy Spirit (conviction of sin, comfort in sorrow, discernment in decisions, power for the believer) and the Bible as God's inerrant and infallible Word to man. Further, this "common salvation" gives definitive moral and ethical mandates regarding man's conduct personally, toward God and others.

It is a certain faith, absolutely authentic, trustworthy and reliable (Jude 3a and 2 Peter 1:20–21). Luke wrote the Gospel of Luke to affirm that the tenets and teachings of the faith may be believed with all "certainty" (Luke 1:1–4). Spurgeon says of Scripture, "These words come from Him who can make no mistake and who can have no wish to deceive His creatures. If I did not believe in the infallibility of the Book, I would rather be without it."[247]

It is a contested faith. "Enemy occupied territory—that is what the world is."[248] And the enemy prowls the earth seeking "to steal, and to kill, and to destroy" (John 10:10) anything and everything that pertains to the Christian faith. Liberalism and heresy threaten its purity, influence and propagation (Jude 4), while governments seek to silence and/or eradicate it. Erwin Lutzer writes, "Many tsunamis are coming against the church today. The pressure to compromise and redefine the Gospel by finding a 'middle way' might well undermine 'the faith which was once delivered unto the saints' (Jude 3). As contemporary culture grows more intolerant of historic Christianity, the church is lured into accommodation and ends up being absorbed by the world. The lamp flickers; then the light goes out."[249] Christians, at the risk of persecution, must wake up, stand up, speak up and shore up (strengthen) "the things which remain" before it's too late (Revelation 3:2).

It is a combative faith, worthy of suffering and dying for. To be silent for whatever reason to the advancement of anti-biblical legislation, cultural biblical antagonism, and liberal religious ideologies is deplorable. It's imperative that Christians mobilize and fight for the preservation (and restoration) of that which is right morally, ethically, politically and biblically. This in essence is the message of Jude. He says, "I want to encourage you to fight hard for the faith that was given the holy people of God" (Jude 3 NCV). Criswell says, "Jude believed that the foundational tenets of the Christian faith were under attack. Nothing but vigorous counter-contention would be sufficient."[250] That same robust and passionate "fight" against the antagonists of the Christian faith (Jude 7–16) is imperative more now than ever. We must not be passive while the bedrock of our faith is under vicious assault. No aberration of the truth must go unchallenged or one iota of religious liberty permitted to be abolished. Chuck Colson wrote, "We must defend the very concept of truth."[251] See John 17:17. Contend earnestly for the faith, not with bigoted zeal or bitterness or self-devised weapons (2 Corinthians 10:4) or feebleness, but courageously, graciously and appropriately (Titus 2:10) in the might of God. MacArthur says, "Wage war against error in all forms and fight strenuously for the truth."[252] Defend the faith as soldiers entrusted to guard a holy and priceless treasure (1 Timothy 6:12).[253]

Luther said, "If I profess with loudest voice and clearest exposition every portion of the truth of God except precisely that little point which the world and the Devil are at the moment attacking, I am not a confessing Christian."[254] He (Luther) serves as our example in giving defense for the faith. To the tribunal at the Imperial Diet of Worms, boldly and unapologetically he said, "Since your majesty and your lordships desire a simple reply, I will answer without horns and without teeth. Unless I am convicted by Scripture and plain reason—I do not accept the authority of popes and councils, for they have contradicted each other—my conscience is captive to the Word of God. I cannot and I will not recant anything, for to go against conscience is neither right nor safe. Here I stand; I cannot do otherwise. God help me. Amen." See Philippians 2:16.

It is a conquering faith. The risk of stumbling in the face of persecution for combating evil looms great. But the divine strength of Omnipotent God is able to preserve (garrison about, guard, protect) the believer, enabling them to conquer. Jude says that God "is able to keep you from falling [stumbling, caving to the pressures of liberalism, damnable heresies, false teachers and the contagion of sin], and to present you faultless [blameless] before the presence of his glory with exceeding joy" (Jude 24). Paul attests the same: "in all these things [antagonisms and temptations of Satan and the world] we are more than conquerors through him that loved us" (Romans 8:37). God is willing and more than able to enable us to "stand" in the face of fierce opposition and persecution for "Christ's name's sake." But we must request His help and rely upon it. See Philippians 4:13. S. D. Gordon says that in persecution repeat the

victor's name (Jesus) into Satan's ears and insist on his retreat.[255]
See Revelation 12:11.

> We rest on thee, our Shield and our Defender!
> We go not forth alone against the foe.
> Strong in thy strength, safe in thy keeping tender,
> We rest on thee; and in Thy name we go.

> We go in faith, our own great weakness feeling
> And needing more each day thy grace to know;
> Yet from our hearts a song of triumph pealing:
> "We rest on thee, and in Thy name we go."

> We rest on thee, our Shield and our Defender!
> Thine is the battle; thine shall be the praise.
> When passing through the gates of pearly splendor,
> Victors, we rest with Thee through endless days.
>
> ~ Edith G. Cherry (1895)

18
Serenity in Suffering

"I may not understand [my persecution] at the moment, but I refuse to become panicky. ...No sorrow will ever disturb me, no trial will ever alarm me, no circumstance will cause me to fret, for I shall rest in the joy of what my Lord is. That is the rest of victory."[256]

~ Alan Redpath

Peace in the fire comes with time in learning its sources. Paul was content (at peace) with being persecuted for the sake of Christ's name and therefore bore it patiently (1 Corinthians 4:12). But he says it was something that had to be cultivated and developed by instruction and experience ("I have learned," Philippians 4:11). Based upon the tense of "have," this learning was continual over a period of time, being initiated at his conversion.[257] Paul's contentment in persecution serves as our example.

He learned to be content by the enablement of Christ's power. Paul said, "I have learned to be content, whatever the circumstances may be. I know now how to live when things are difficult and I know how to live when things are prosperous. In general and in particular I have learned the secret of facing either poverty or plenty. I am ready for anything through the strength of the one who lives within me." (Philippians 4:12–13 PHILLIPS). Continuously abiding in Christ and relying upon His power to meet every adverse circumstance of life victoriously is the secret of true contentment. See John 15:5, 11.

He learned to be content by exhibiting trust in God's plan. Whatever befalls believers is orchestrated or allowed by sovereign God for their best and His glory. Jeremiah testifies to that truth: "'For I know the plans I have for you,' declares the LORD, 'plans to prosper you and not to harm you, plans to give you hope and a future'" (Jeremiah 29:11 NIV). "Contentedness requires that we should believe our condition, whatever it may be, to be determined by God, or at least that He permits it according to His pleasure."[258] To trust God implicitly brings contentment inexplicable. Joseph Parker said,

"'Abraham believed God' (Romans 4:3) and said to his eyes, 'Stand back!' and to the laws of nature, 'Hold your peace!' and to an unbelieving heart, 'Silence, you lying tempter!' He simply 'believed God.'"[259] Saith Spurgeon, "Believing that God rules all, that He governs wisely, that He brings good out of evil, the believer's heart is assured, and he is enabled calmly to meet each trial as it comes."[260]

He learned to be content through hope that was infused into his soul from the Holy Scriptures. Contentment is accompanied with and inseparable from hope for deliverance, relief, and rescue, either in the present life or in the world to come. The psalmist said, "I wait for the LORD, my soul doth wait, and in his word do I hope" (Psalm 130:5). See Psalm 102:28. The hope of Heaven, a glorified body free from the throes of persecution, reunion with the saints, eternity in a domain free from sin and evil, and continuous fellowship with the Lord all infuse hope that yields peace, calm, and contentment in life's struggles. And from whence does this hope come? Paul says, "Faith cometh by hearing, and hearing by the Word of God" (Romans 10:17).

He learned to be content through the hardships of life. Paul gained invaluable lessons from times of pain (a hard schoolmaster) that made him more serene in each successive hardship and made it easier to bear. See 2 Corinthians 11:24–27. The exercise of faith and its proven effectiveness produce greater faith in facing persecution. The Bible says, "And not only this, but [with joy] let us exult in our sufferings and rejoice in our hardships, knowing that hardship (distress, pressure, trouble) produces patient endurance; and endurance, proven character (spiritual maturity); and proven character, hope and confident assurance [of eternal salvation]. Such hope [in God's promises] never disappoints us, because God's love has been abundantly poured out within our hearts through the Holy Spirit who was given to us" (Romans 5:3–5 AMP).

Ye fearful saints, fresh courage take;
  The clouds you so much dread
Are big with mercy and shall break
  With blessings on your head.

~ William Cowper (1773)

Doubtlessly, Paul also learned how to be content through observing saints that in the fire of affliction and trouble stood firm, confident, patient, and joyous. See Chapter 19, *Company of the Persecuted.*

19
Company of the Persecuted

"We rejoice that righteousness is so dear to us that we are willing to suffer for its sake, and that we are counted worthy to suffer in the best company."[261]

~ *J. A. Macdonald*

The Christian's identification with biblical martyrs (Hebrews 11) is honorable, motivational, and inspirational. What an impressive company with which to be associated! Hebrews 12:1 indicates that the persecuted heroes of the faith of Hebrews 11 encourage believers to "hold fast" (Hebrews 10:23; Hebrews 3:6) under the rod of persecution as well as keep their own suffering in perspective (Hebrews 11:10–16; Romans 8:28). The text reads, "Therefore, since we are surrounded by such a great cloud of witnesses, let us throw off everything that hinders and the sin that so easily entangles. And let us run with perseverance the race marked out for us" (NIV).

"Wherefore" or "therefore" (reference back to chapter 11 which cites 18 heroes of the faith) "seeing we" (saints of earth) also are "compassed about" (encircled about) with so great a "cloud" ("figure of speech indicating a large group"[262]) "of witnesses" (the people of Chapter 11 whom God commended for constancy of faith). Kenneth Wuest states, "The word [witnesses] does not include in its meaning the idea of a person *looking at something.*"[263] Donald Hagner agrees, stating, "'Witnesses' here does not mean observers of the present conduct of Christians, but rather those who testify or give evidence of the victorious life of faith."[264] ("We are watching them for encouragement rather than them watching us in examination."[265]) It was reflection upon their faith that enabled persevering endurance in persecution "for Christ's sake," and we are inspired to do likewise.

Therefore, when facing gigantic problems, remember David who slew Goliath. In times of tumultuous trials, remember

Shadrach, Meshach, and Abed-nego who survived the fiery furnace. Upon embarking upon the unknown in service to God, remember Abraham and be encouraged. In times of false accusations, remember Joseph in Potiphar's jail. In seasons of affliction and persecution for the Gospel's sake, remember Moses in Pharaoh's house. In times of being under an anti-God regime, remember Gideon's strong confidence in God to deliver Israel from the hands of the cruel and evil Midianites. In moments of battle against superior forces in number and power, remember Samson that relied confidently upon God for abnormal strength to war against them victoriously. When beckoned to protect or make provision for saints that are being pursued by forces hostile to the cause of Christ, remember Rahab's trust in God by the hiding of two spies in her house in Jericho at the risk of her own safety. In refuting unrighteousness and proclaiming God's Word, remember the prophets who demonstrated strong confidence in the truth, even if it was unwelcome, and who delivered it, depending upon God courageously and dauntlessly, even at the risk of their lives. Remember; and in remembering, be encouraged, uplifted, inspired and motivated to press onward in the race, regardless of the obstacles Satan hurls upon you. Let the Heavenly saints cheer you on to the finish line!

Persecuted saints outside the Bible also exemplify how believers, if called upon, are to suffer and die for Christ and His cause. See Chapter 30, *Tortured for Christ*.

Elijah, after Mount Carmel, mistakenly believed that he was the last prophet standing for God (Romans 11:3). But he was wrong, for there were yet 7,000 men that had not bowed the knee unto Baal (Romans 11:4). Don't allow the plight to blind your sight to the vast company of mighty warriors, past and present, that stand and suffer with you.

Let the saints new anthems raise;
    Wake the morn with gladness.
God Himself, to joy and praise,
    Turns the martyrs' sadness.

This the day that won their crown,
    Opened heaven's bright portal,
As they laid the mortal down
    And put on the immortal.

Never flinched they from the flame,
    From the torture, never;
Vain the foeman's sharpest aim,
    Satan's best endeavor.

For by faith they saw the land,
    Decked in all its glory,
Where triumphant now they stand
    With the victor's story.

Faith they had that knew not shame,
    Love that could not languish;
And eternal hope o'ercame
    That one moment's anguish.

Up and follow, Christian men!
    Press through toil and sorrow!
Spurn the night of fear, and then,
    Oh, the glorious morrow!

~ Joseph of the Studium (c. 820)

20
Readiness to Combat Persecution

"The trumpet still plays the notes of war. You cannot sit down and put the victory wreath on your head. You do not have a crown. You still must wear the helmet and carry the sword. You must watch, pray, and fight. Expect your last battle to be most difficult, for the enemy's fiercest charge is reserved for the end of the day."[266]
~ C. H. Spurgeon

"If you are going to walk with Jesus Christ," writes George Whitefield, "you are going to be opposed."[267] J. C. Ryle well said, "No Christian is in a healthy state of mind who is not prepared for persecution. He that expects to cross the troubled waters of this world and to reach Heaven with wind and tide always in his favor, knows nothing yet as he ought to know. We can never know what is before us in this life. But of one thing we may be very sure—we must carry the cross if we would wear the crown."[268]

Calvin remarks, "But if, at any time, the Lord spares our weakness and does not permit the ungodly to torment us as they would desire, yet, during the season of repose and leisure, it is proper for us to meditate on this doctrine, that we may be ready, whenever it shall be necessary, to enter the field and may not engage in the contest till we have been well prepared."[269] Saith Spurgeon, "Since our Lord has forewarned us, it is well for us to stand ready for the trial which He predicts and to ask ourselves whether we are ready to bear oppression for Christ's sake."[270]

What ought the saint to do to prepare for persecution?

Realize its likelihood. Prepare for its actuality. John MacArthur said, "Many of us will never taste the kind of persecution that the apostles or the brothers overseas have known. But the willingness to endure sacrifice for the sake of Christ should never be far from our thinking."[271] John Calvin said, "Happy are they who suffer persecution. The disciples of Christ have very great need of this instruction; and the harder and more disagreeable it is for the flesh to admit it, the more earnestly ought we to make it the subject of our meditation."[272]

Engage in earnest prayer. If believers are uncompromisingly and perseveringly to stand for Christ when persecution comes, they must rediscover the power of prayer.[273] Jesus said, "Watch ye therefore, and pray always, that ye may be accounted worthy to escape all these things that shall come to pass, and to stand before the Son of man" (Luke 21:36). We stand the tallest when we kneel the longest. Thomas à Kempis says: "Shut thy door upon thee and call unto Jesus thy love. When Jesus is nigh, all goodness is nigh, and nothing seemeth hard; but when He is not nigh, all things are hard. If Jesus speaks one word, there is great comfort. To be without Jesus is a grievous Hell, and to be with Jesus is a sweet Paradise."

S. D. Gordon said, "The enemy yields only what he must. He yields only what is taken. Therefore, the ground must be taken step by step. Prayer must be definite. He yields only when he must. Therefore, the prayer must be persistent. He continually renews his attacks, therefore the ground taken must be *held* against him in the Victor's name."[274] R. A. Torrey said, "All that God is and all that God has is at the disposal of prayer. Prayer can do anything that God can do; and as God can do everything, prayer is omnipotent."[275]

The preacher George Allen Smith was standing on the precipice of a mountain in the Alps viewing Switzerland when a gushing wind suddenly arose that threatened to blow him over the edge. Immediately his guide cried out, "Mr. Smith! On your knees, sir! The only way you're safe up here is on your knees!" In battling opposition to Christ, the only way you're safe down here is on your knees. Recall that when persecution arose, Daniel didn't have to adjust his prayer life; he prayed three times a day as was his habit. It was this devout habit of prayer that prepared him for the persecution of the king and enabled his perseverance through it (Daniel 6:10). Let us do as Daniel and make preparation for persecution by frequent and fervent dialogue with God.

Absorb the Holy Scripture. The Bible says, "Stand therefore, having girded your waist with truth" (Ephesians 6:14 NKJV) and by taking up the "the sword of the Spirit, which is the word of God" (verse 17). Assimilate and memorize the Word that you might have biblical texts at your command to use in rebuttal of heresy and in defense of the Gospel. Albert Barnes says, "A single text of Scripture is better to meet a temptation [opposition, hostile forces] than all the philosophy which the world contains. The tempter can reason, and reason plausibly too. But he cannot resist a direct and positive command of the Almighty."[276]

Fix your mind on Christ. Spurgeon said, "There have never been 15 minutes in my life when I did not sense the presence of Christ." Keep your heart focused upon Christ constantly (Hebrews 12:2). It is as much a mental as it is a spiritual discipline. "It is not a single, unrepeated act that He wishes here to enforce, but a holy habit of soul. As the gaze of the mariner steering his vessel through perilous seas is perpetually fixed upon the compass, so we, voyaging to eternity through the treacherous waters of time, must have eye and heart centered on Christ as the sole director of our progress. The word expresses a continuous and sustained action of the inner man. But it does more. It not only means 'looking,' as the translation gives it, but looking off or away. We are taught to look away from all else to 'Jesus only.'"[277]

Rely upon the name of the Lord. "Our help is in the name of the LORD, who made heaven and earth" (Psalm 124:8). B. H. Carroll said, "'In the name' stood for all that Christ was and taught. During grave persecution (the Dark Ages) in the early church when saints were pursued for torture and death, they would knock at doors and say, 'In the Name.' The Christian who answered the knock would recognize the password and give refuge at the risk of his own life. Christian literature likewise was distributed in this manner."[278]

Persecuted saints of that era literally relied upon the name of the Lord for their safety and successes over hostile powers. C. H. Spurgeon states, "Our warfare is with evil within us and around us, and we ought to be persuaded that we are able to get the victory and that we shall do so *in the name of the Lord* Jesus. We are not riding for a fall, but to win; and win we shall. The grace of God in its omnipotence is put forth for the overflow of evil in every form— hence the certainty of triumph."[279] History affirms that persecuted saints by faith "in the name of the Lord" victoriously endured the cruel and inhumane treatment exacted upon them. See Hebrews 11:4–38. And even so may we. In this vein, Kyle Yates is correct to say, "A man's belief about God largely determines his conduct"[280]—and endurance in opposition.

Be controlled by the Holy Spirit. Walk in entire surrender, subordination to the authority of the Holy Spirit, and in His infilling of strength and power (Galatians 5:16; Ephesians 5:18). We are only equal to the challenges of the day (including persecution, should it befall us) through the power given from God by the Holy Spirit (Acts 1:8).

Cultivate your relationship with Christ. That notable counsel of Eliphaz to Job: "Acquaint now thyself with him [God], and be at peace" (Job 22:21), is applicable to all believers. Saith the NASB Dictionary, it means to be *intimately acquainted*.[281] Some believers know Christ more with their head than their heart. Billy Graham said, "If you are not strengthening the inner man or woman by daily walking with God now, when a crisis comes you will quake with fear and give in, having no strength to stand up for Christ."[282]

Clothe yourself with the armor of God. To *stand firm* against the coming persecution, dress daily in the armor of God (Ephesians 6:10–18). Martyn Lloyd-Jones states, "If you are to be a soldier in this army, if you are to fight victoriously in this crusade, you have to put on the entire equipment given to you. That is a rule in any army,…And that is infinitely truer in this spiritual realm and warfare with which we are concerned,…because your understanding is inadequate. It is God alone who knows your enemy, and He knows exactly the provision that is essential to you if you are to continue standing. Every single part and portion of this armor is absolutely essential, and the first thing you have to learn is that you are not in a position to pick and choose."[283]

Determine to manifest joy in it. Paul and Silas sang while shackled in a Philippian jail (Acts 16:25–34). G. Campbell Morgan says, "Men who sing while they suffer are men who have learned the profound secret that suffering is the method by which joy is perfected in human life and human history. But again, men who sing in prison are men who cannot be imprisoned. It was impossible to imprison Paul and Silas. But they were imprisoned. They could be shown in that prison, in the inner chamber, with their feet fast in the stocks. Ah, but they were not imprisoned. Fellowship with God is the franchise of eternity. You may put these men within your stone walls, you may make their feet fast in the wood of your brutal stocks, but they are not there. They are sitting with Christ in heavenly places. They are ranging themselves with the living ones. They are swinging the censers of their heavenly priesthood in high and holy places. As to bodily presence, they are there in prison; but as to spiritual essence, they are with God. Men who sing in prison are men who cannot be imprisoned."[284]

Man may bind our hands but not our hearts, silence our tongues but not our songs. Imprisoned Romanian pastor Richard Wurmbrand's captors, despite crushing four of his vertebrae and making eighteen holes in his body, could not defeat him. He testified, "Alone in my cell, cold, hungry, and in rags, I danced for joy every night."[285]

Onward Christian soldiers,
    Marching as to war
With the cross of Jesus
    Going on before!
Christ, the royal Master,
    Leads against the foe;
Forward into battle
    See His banners go!

At the name of Jesus
    Satan's host doth flee;
On then, Christian soldiers,
    On to victory!
Hell's foundations quiver
    At the shout of praise.
Brothers, lift your voices;
    Loud your anthems raise!

Like a mighty army
　　Moves the Church of God;
Brothers, we are treading
　　Where the saints have trod.
We are not divided,
　　All one Body we—
One in faith and Spirit,
　　One eternally.

Crowns and thrones may perish,
　　Kingdoms rise and wane;
But the Church of Jesus
　　Constant will remain.
Gates of Hell can never
　　'Gainst the Church prevail;
We have Christ's own promise,
　　Which can never fail.

Onward, then, ye people,
　　Join our happy throng!
Blend with ours your voices
　　In the triumph song.
Glory, laud and honor
　　Unto Christ, the King;
This through countless ages
　　Men and angels sing.

~ Sabine Baring-Gould (1834–1924)

The bottom line: "We don't determine," says Greg Laurie, "what challenges, what hardships, or what difficulties come our way. All we determine is how we will react to those things when they come."[286] The time to prepare for the coming storm of persecution is today.

21
Response to Persecution

"When a man is called on to suffer something for his Christianity, that is always a crucial moment; it is the great occasion; it is the clash between the world and Christ; it is a moment in the drama of eternity. To have a share in such a moment is not a penalty but a glory. 'Rejoice at such a moment,' says Jesus, 'and be glad.'"[287]
~ *William Barclay*

Scripture reveals three *positive* responses the believer may make in the face of persecution under the leadership of the Holy Spirit. The first positive response to persecution is avoidance. In dispatching the disciples to witness, Jesus said, "When you are persecuted in one place, flee to another" (Matthew 10:23 NIV). What do biblical conservative scholars say is the meaning of the text? Leon Morris remarks, "When a disciple finds one place implacably hostile, it is not his function to continue to offer himself for maltreatment and death; needlessly to court martyrdom is not the Christian way. Jesus tells him to seek safety in flight, to flee to the next town."[288] Matthew Henry, concurring with Morris, writes, "In case of great peril, the disciples of Christ may go out of the way of danger, though they must not go out of the way of duty. No sinful, unlawful means may be used to escape [only that open door the Holy Spirit provides]."[289] Plummer states, "It sometimes happens that there is more real heroism in daring to fly from danger than in stopping to meet it. To stop and meet useless risks because one is afraid of being called a coward is one of the subtlest forms of cowardice, and the desire to be thought brave is not a high motive for courageous action."[290]

> God's Word can go forth powerfully through the unspoken testimony of martyrdom, but it is often better for people to remain alive to speak it aloud.
> C. Bloomberg

Bloomberg comments, "The flip side of encouraging bold testimony under persecution when one has no alternative is the command to flee hostility whenever possible. Jesus calls His followers to bravery but not foolishness. God's Word can go forth powerfully through the unspoken testimony of martyrdom, but it is often better for people to remain alive to speak it aloud."[291]

Flight from fight is justifiable provided it is sanctioned by the Lord. Note, Christ never sanctions flight that brings jeopardy to His cause, people, Word, or glory. Flight that is acceptable unto the Lord ought to be undertaken. There is biblical precedent for the response. God instructed Elijah to avoid persecution by King Ahab by hiding (1 Kings 17:1–6). God told Joseph to flee to Egypt with the Christ-child to avoid persecution (Matthew 2:13–18). The two Jericho spies hid from its wicked King in Rahab's house (Joshua 2:1–4). Paul escaped death in Damascus by being 'let down by the wall in a basket' by the disciples (Acts 9:23–25). Paul and Barnabas, in discovering a plot in Iconium to stone them, fled the town to escape it (Acts 14:5–7). And, as discussed, Jesus instructed the disciples to flee towns and cities that persecuted them (Matthew 10:23). Jesus Himself avoided persecution when it was not of the Father's will (Matthew 12:14–15; Luke 22:42).

Flight over fight, when ordained of the Lord, is not cowardice or merely a means of escape from suffering. (It *is* cowardice when done for the sake of comfort and safety rather than "for Christ's sake" and outside of His direction.) It is to permit the continuance of uninhibited ministry, perhaps a more successful one. *Flight* preserves *fight* to spread the *light.*

> Flight preserves fight to spread the light.

Souls were saved in Lystra and Derbe because Paul and Barnabas fled persecution in Iconium into those towns (Acts 14:7). That in itself doesn't justify flight from persecution, but it does reveal why the Lord prompts believers at times to avoid it. "There are occasions when the duty is rather to spread the message than to seal it with death or to have one's lips closed by imprisonment. But only 'he that is spiritual' (1 Corinthians 2:15) will be able to understand which course of action the special circumstances require."[292]

Ignatius of Antioch wrongly desired persecution and urged the Roman church not to deny him the fate.[293] He said to that Roman congregation, "For I am afraid of your love, in that it may do me wrong; for it is easy for you to do what you want, but it is difficult for me to reach God, unless you spare me [don't interfere with my execution]."[294] He pleaded with them to let him be "food for the wild beasts, through whom I can reach God."[295] It was through persecution (imitation of Christ's suffering and martyrdom) that Ignatius thought spiritual progression (true perfection[296]) and likeness to Christ advanced. Flawed theology refuses to shun persecution, even when that is ordained of Christ.

Shrewd forethought governed by the Holy Spirit must be exhibited in the means (how, when, where) of avoiding persecution (when allowable and directed by the Lord). For example, when Christians faced persecution in Tertullian's time (A.D. 155–220), he advised them to limit attendees at worship to a small group ("a church of threes") and to meet at night, for "it is better that you sometimes should not see your crowds, than subject yourselves (to a tribute bondage)."[297] In avoidance of persecution, therefore, 'be as wise as a serpent, and harmless as doves' (Matthew 10:16). See Chapter 13, *Reaction to Persecution*.

The second positive response to persecution is endurance. When avoidance of persecution is not optional or forbidden by the Holy Spirit, the saint must steadfastly stand firm in that place, even unto death. Spurgeon says, "Perseverance is the target of all our spiritual enemies. Satan will make many a fierce attack on your perseverance; it will be the mark for all his arrows. He will strive to hinder you in service…make you weary of suffering, or attack your steadfastness. Wear your shield, Christian, therefore, close upon your armor, and cry mightily unto God, that by his Spirit you may endure to the end."[298] See 2 Timothy 2:3. A biblical example of this response to oppression is that of Shadrach, Meshach, and Abed-nego, who refused to bow before King Nebuchadnezzar's golden image, fully realizing the consequences (Daniel 3:8–30). See Chapter 32, *Victors and Heroes*.

The third positive response to persecution is resistance. Legal resistance to persecution through use of the law is sometimes appropriate. Jesus gave defense of His innocence at His trial (John 18:23). Paul utilized the law to avoid persecution (Acts 16:36–39; 22:24–29; 25:10–11). Like fleeing, resisting is permissible, provided it does not undermine the mission of God at play.[299] "Christian resistance to religious persecution must not distort, diminish or contradict the Gospel, God's purposes in persecution, Christ's mission in the world, or the Holy Spirit's leading to respond to persecution in another manner."[300] Thomas Schirrmacher states, "Christians are loyal citizens who seek the welfare of their state, country and people; but whenever the State tries to force them to dishonor God, they must obey God more than man (Acts 5:29)."[301]

There are four *wrong* responses the believer may make in facing persecution. The first wrong response to persecution is compliance. Though the heart says one thing, the mouth confesses another and denies Christ, as Peter did to the damsel (John 18:17).

The second wrong response to persecution is compromise. To pacify the persecutor and to escape persecution, concessions are made regarding belief and practice. See Galatians 6:12. Remember the challenge of Elijah: "If the LORD be God, follow him; but if Baal, then follow him" (1 Kings 18:21). There is no justification for compromise with regard to one's faith in Jesus Christ as Lord and Savior and His Word as being the sole authority by which man must live. There is no middle ground; it's either God or Baal. Jesus said, "No one can be loyal to two masters. He is bound to hate one and love the other, or support one and despise the other" (Matthew 6:24 PHILLIPS). Adrian Rogers said, "There is a way you can escape persecution: just fail to be salt and light. Just compromise. Be conformed to this world, and you won't get any persecution" (Matthew 5:13–14).[302] Jesus said, "If any man will come after me, let him deny himself, and take up his cross, and follow me" (Matthew 16:24).

> We must all decide here and now where we stand. Will we pivot or will we hold fast?
> Albert Mohler, Jr.

The third wrong response to persecution is cowardice. Saith Billy Graham, "Thousands of Christians compromise their faith in Jesus Christ by denying Him. Even some clergymen neglect or deliberately refuse to close a public prayer in the name of Jesus for fear of offending an unbeliever. They cannot endure the persecution that may follow an acknowledgement of Jesus Christ."[303] Others stand firm at the outset, only to yield cowardly to the threat of severer affliction afterwards. "We do not seem to have the fearless courage in us today to stand before a sinful, gainsaying, and Christ-rejecting world," states Criswell. "We mollify our witness, and we compromise with the evil in the world. It is a rare person who will stand up and say the truth at a price. It is so much easier for us to say sweet, complimentary and compromising words rather than oppose evil, unbelief, rejection, sin, wrong and iniquity. The Lord said, 'Woe unto you when all men speak well of you'—when everyone has a tendency to praise you. They do so because you are not opposing their sin. You are not standing up for what is right, and you are not presenting the truth of God as it is in Christ Jesus."[304]

Don't be numbered among the "fearful" (Revelation 21:8). It is noble to standfast at the first, but it's far nobler to endure to the end.

The fourth wrong response to persecution is collapse. The "believer" blatantly denies the faith, abandons Christ, proving that he was a believer in name only (1 John 2:19). In Jesus' parable of the seeds, the seed that was planted in a stony place shot up with promise of great fruitfulness, only to perish when the burning heat of the sun rose upon it. "Some seed fell on the stony ground. That is like a person who hears the message and right away he is glad to hear it. But it does not go down deep in his heart. He believes it for a short time. When trouble or a hard time comes because of the message, he stops believing" (Matthew 13:20–21 WE).

Spurgeon says, "To give up religion because of persecution is to prefer ourselves to Christ, to be selfish enough to regard our own ease rather than His glory, to consult our own peace rather than His honor, though we have said that we love Him beyond all else for redeeming us by His blood. It will show that we love Him not at all, but are ungrateful, false, and hypocritical."[305]

The believer's only proper response to persecution is to *cling to the Cross of Christ.*

So I'll cherish the old rugged cross,
    Till my trophies at last I lay down;
I will cling to the old rugged cross
    And exchange it some day for a crown.

Oh, that old rugged cross, so despised by the world,
    Has a wondrous attraction for me;
For the dear Lamb of God left His glory above
    To bear it to dark Calvary.

In that old rugged cross, stained with blood so divine,
    A wondrous beauty I see,
For 'twas on that old cross Jesus suffered and died
    To pardon and sanctify me.

To that old rugged cross I will ever be true,
    Its shame and reproach gladly bear;
Then He'll call me someday to my home far away,
    Where His glory forever I'll share.

~ George Bennard (1913)

Albert Mohler, Jr., forthrightly said, "We must all decide here and now where we stand. Will we pivot or will we hold fast?"[306]

22
Persecution and the Apostle Paul

"The persecuted are not merely men who have passed through a certain experience, but men who bear abiding traces of it in their character. They are marked men, and bear the stamp of trial on their faces. It arrests the notice of the passer-by: commands his respect, and prompts the question, Who and whence? They are veteran soldiers of righteousness with an unmistakable air of dignity, serenity, and buoyancy about them."[307]

~ W. Robertson Nicoll

The persecution Paul suffered and its *marks* borne out of loyalty to Christ reveal instructional and inspirational truths. Paul says that allegiance to Christ leads to persecution, which inscribes on the body its telltale marks. "For I bear in my body the marks of the Lord Jesus" (Galatians 6:17). See 2 Corinthians 11:23–33. Paul's life bore "marks" of utmost devotion and allegiance to Christ. Slaves in biblical days were often branded with the "mark" of their master, showing ownership; Paul's numerous "scars" (beatings, stonings, shipwreck, imprisonment, hardships, shame) suffered in behalf of Christ were "marks" or "brands" showing ownership of Jesus Christ. See Philemon 1:1 and Revelation 2:10.

William Barclay suggests "Like Mr. Valiant-for-Truth, Paul said, 'My marks and scars I carry with me to be my witness to him who will now be my rewarder.'"[308] "He was stamped and marked by life. The wounds of his conflicts, the furrows of his years, were on him. And all these wounds and furrows had come to him since the great change of his life. They were closely bound up with the service of his Master, to whom he had given himself at Damascus. Every scar must have still quivered with the earnestness of the words of Christian loyalty which brought the blow that made it."[309] Paul's vivid description of the "marks" borne for Christ may be likened to that of Antipater (Herod's father") in *Josephus, War 1:97,* where he disrobes and reveals his many scars as witnesses to his loyalty to Caesar.[310]

Christ's loyal followers, like Paul, will bear marks of persecution (hardship and suffering). So saith Paul: "We are troubled on every side, yet not distressed; we are perplexed, but not in despair; Persecuted, but not forsaken; cast down, but not destroyed; *Always bearing* about in the body the dying of the Lord Jesus, that the life also of Jesus might be made manifest in our body" (2 Corinthians 4:8–10). It's an impossibility to love Christ supremely and not suffer for it (Matthew 5:11–12). It's the marks inflicted, not the medals awarded, that testify to undying allegiance to Christ. Hendriksen said, "Scars are the price which every believer pays for his loyalty to Christ."[311] Christ bore the marks of agonizing torment and suffering for us—the nail prints in His hands and feet, sword-pierced side, bleeding brow with crown of jagged thorns, scar-riddled back by flogging with the Roman cat-o'-nine-tails, mocking, hostility, imprisonment and execution upon the Cross. With Paul, let us bear our marks of love for Him.

> When I survey the wondrous cross
> On which the Prince of glory died,
> My richest gain I count but loss
> And pour contempt on all my pride.
>
> See from His head, His hands, His feet,
> Sorrow and love flow mingled down!
> Did e'er such love and sorrow meet
> Or thorns compose so rich a crown?
>
> Were the whole realm of nature mine,
> That were a present far too small;
> Love so amazing, so divine,
> Demands my soul, my life, my all.
>
> ~ Isaac Watts (1707)

What truths might be learned from Paul's marks (experiences with persecution)? Paul says the form and intensity of persecution (suffering borne and its "marks" manifested) is determined by the believer's level of allegiance to Christ. Such is inferred in Paul's words to young Timothy: "Indeed, all who delight in *pursuing* righteousness and are determined to live godly lives in Christ Jesus will be hunted and persecuted [because of their faith]" (2 Timothy 3:12 AMP). That is, the greater the pursuit of righteousness, the greater the hostility and hardship. Paul suffered much because he pursued the honor and glory of Christ vigorously and constantly in preaching (the unadulterated Gospel, Acts 20:27; Romans 1:16), practice (nonconformity to the world, 2 Corinthians 6:17), passion (to know Christ intimately and make Him known to everyone, Philippians 3:10), pleasure (to be well-pleasing to Christ, 2 Corinthians 5:9; Philippians 1:21), and posture (unwavering steadfastness in conviction, despite the consequence, 2 Corinthians 11:23–33).

Paul says that persecution, although painful, is pleasurable. Paradoxically, Paul found pleasure in persecution. He testified, "Therefore, I take *pleasure* in infirmities, in reproaches, in necessities, in persecutions, in distresses for Christ's sake" (2 Corinthians 12:10). The word "pleasure" means "something chosen gladly," "to count good," "to approve" and "to delight in." Believers are to bear the reproach of Christ heartily and delightfully, regardless of the cost or consequence, knowing it honors Christ and promotes His cause.

John MacArthur points out that "Paul took no pleasure in the pain itself but rejoiced in the power of Christ that it revealed through him."[312] Albert Barnes said, it's "no doubt that Paul, in the midst of all his infirmities and reproaches, had a joy above that which all the wealth and honor of the world could give. See here the power of religion. It not only supports; it comforts. It not only enables one to bear suffering with resignation, but it enables him to rejoice. Philosophy blunts the feelings; infidelity leaves people to complain and repine in trial. The pleasures of this world have no power even to support or comfort in times of affliction, but Christianity furnishes positive pleasure in trial and enables the sufferer to smile through his tears."[313] See James 1:2 and I Peter 4:13. Spurgeon says, "Thus to you as to Samson, out of the eater cometh forth meat, and out of the strong cometh forth sweetness. This lion roars upon you, but the day shall come when you will find honey in it and bless the name of the

Lord."[314] "Paul and Silas made the prison walls ring with praise, though their backs were livid with scars and stained by blood."[315]

Paul says that persecution inflicted for Christ's glory is not loss but gain (profitable). The believer in persecution is made stronger instead of weaker. So saith Paul in 2 Corinthians 12:10. Matthew Henry comments, *"When I am weak, then am I strong.* This is a Christian paradox: when we are weak in ourselves, then we are strong in the grace of our Lord Jesus Christ; when we see ourselves weak in ourselves, then we go out of ourselves to Christ and are qualified to receive strength from Him and experience most of the supplies of divine strength and grace."[316] "Affliction, meekly borne, hath a refining power; it elevates and refines the whole character. Faith is strengthened by trials; patience is acquired by the habit of enduring affliction. Without endurance, without suffering, there is no opportunity of developing the grace of patience."[317] See Romans 5:3–5. Paul's imprisonment and persecution were means of his sanctification and edification.

Paul says that persecution offers the opportunity to witness to one's persecutors. Paul witnessed to King Agrippa and Festus (Acts 26:19–29). When he was under "house arrest" in Rome, "there came many to him into his lodging; to whom he expounded and testified the kingdom of God, persuading them concerning Jesus, both out of the law of Moses, and out of the prophets, from morning till evening" (Acts 28:23). They regularly changed the guard chained to Paul, providing a sure audience for the Gospel. During the two years of Paul's imprisonment, soldiers watched him write or dictate letters to the Ephesian, Philippian, and Colossian churches and to Philemon (a witness in and of itself), and listened to his sermons. And both contributed to the salvation of some in "Caesar's household" (Philippians 4:22). See Philippians 1:12–13 and Matthew 10:18. "The mass of men," writes Albert Barnes, "will somehow see in the endurance of Christian martyrs an argument for the Divine origin of their religion. The number has been so great, they have borne their sufferings so patiently, they have met death so calmly, so many of them have been distinguished for intelligence, and so many of them were witnesses of what they affirmed to be true, that the general impression on mankind is that sufferings so varied, so protracted, so meekly borne, could be only in the cause of truth."[318] Adrian Rogers said, "Indeed, your scars may be your greatest ministry. Just as the scars of Jesus convinced Thomas, perhaps your scars will convince someone today."[319]

> Your scars may be your greatest ministry. Just as the scars of Jesus convinced Thomas, perhaps your scars will convince someone today.
> Adrian Rogers

Paul says that persecution gives the believer the opportunity to share in Christ's suffering. He states, "Now if we are children, then we are heirs—heirs of God and co-heirs with Christ, if indeed we share in his sufferings in order that we may also share in his glory" (Romans 8:17 NIV). Peter similarly says, "Dear friends, don't be surprised at the fiery trials you are going through, as if something strange were happening to you. Instead, be very glad—for these trials make you partners with Christ in his suffering, so that you will have the wonderful joy of seeing his glory when it is revealed to all the world" (1 Peter 4:12–13 NLT). As we endeavor to fulfill Christ's redemptive purpose, suffering will be inevitable, even as it was for Him in its introductory revelation and proclamation. See John 1:11; Luke 22:63–65; and John 19:16–19. The suffering, Paul says, is trivial in comparison to the glory that awaits us in Heaven (Romans 8:17b and 2 Corinthians 4:17). See Chapter 8, *Motivation for Suffering Persecution.*

Paul says that Christ's grace provides a placidness and power in the face of persecution. To Paul, Christ said, "My grace is sufficient for you" (2 Corinthians 12:9 NIV). Despite the pain and agony suffered in persecution, Paul possessed a refreshing peace and strength that was enabled by Christ's amazing grace. "Christ assures Paul that the supply of his grace…for the bearing of the pain and buffeting would never run dry. He needed nothing more than Christ's grace. Having that, he had the strength to endure all things (1 Corinthians 13:7) and to do all things to the glory of God

(1 Corinthians 10:31). In Philippians 4:13 he later encapsulates his own response to this promise of complete sufficiency: 'I am strong enough to meet all circumstances through my union with him who strengthens me.'[320]

> In vain the powers of darkness try
> To work the Church's ill;
> The Friend of sinners reigns on high
> And checks them at His will.
>
> My trust is in His grace alone;
> His house shall be my home.
> How sweet His mercies past to own
> And hope for more to come.
>
> ~ Henry F. Lyte (1833)

Christ's grace is the saint's sufficiency in suffering perseveringly and peacefully. It's His grace that is capable of enabling one to endure in the direst of conditions or circumstances. Whatever comfort you require, His grace is sufficient to bestow it; whatever the difficulty is, His grace is sufficient to uphold you; whatever the sorrow you have, His grace is sufficient to sustain you; whatever the fear might be, His grace is sufficient to conquer it; whatever anxiety you feel, His grace is sufficient to thwart it; whatever the service called for, His grace is sufficient to enable it; whatever gloom there is, His grace is sufficient to dispel it; whatever torture is inflicted, His grace is sufficient to bear it; and whatever danger is confronted, His grace is sufficient to deliver you from it or sustain you in it. Matthew Henry says, "Christ Jesus understands our case and knows our need and will proportion the remedy to our malady and not only strengthen us, but glorify Himself."[321]

> From over hill and plain
> There comes the signal strain—
>   'Tis loyalty, loyalty, loyalty to Christ
> Its music rolls along;
> The hills take up the song
>   Of loyalty, loyalty, yes, loyalty to Christ.

"On to victory! On to victory!"
Cries our great Commander, "On!"
We'll move at His command;
We'll soon possess the land
Thru loyalty, loyalty, yes, loyalty to Christ!

Oh, hear, ye brave, the sound
That moves the earth around—
   'Tis loyalty, loyalty, loyalty to Christ.
Arise to dare and do;
Ring out the watchword true
   Of loyalty, loyalty, yes, loyalty to Christ.

Come, join our loyal throng—
We'll rout the giant wrong—
   'Tis loyalty, loyalty, loyalty to Christ.
Where Satan's banners float,
We'll send the bugle note
   Of loyalty, loyalty, yes, loyalty to Christ.

                    ~ Elijah T. Cassel (1894)

23
Endurance to the End

"Perseverance is the badge of true saints. Satan will make many a fierce attack on your perseverance; it will be the mark for all his arrows."[322]

~ C. H. Spurgeon

"But he that shall endure unto the end, the same shall be saved" (Matthew 24:13). See Matthew 10:22. It is not the perseverance in persecution (trials, tribulations, trouble for His name's sake) that gains salvation; rather, it's that which confirms and authenticates it. Those that fall away (do not endure persecution unto the end, abandon the faith) give proof that they never were saved. John says, "These 'against-Christ' people used to be members of our churches, but they never really belonged with us or else they would have stayed. When they left us it proved that they were not of us at all" (1 John 2:19 TLB). "The persecution for the *Word's* sake" purges the church of mere "professors," those in whom the saving grace of Christ never took root (Matthew 13:20–21).

Matthew Henry comments, *"Persecuting times are discovering times. Wolves in sheep's clothing will then throw off their disguise and appear wolves. Perseverance wins the crown, through free grace, and shall wear it."*[323]

"Endurance [perseverance, tenacity, steadfastness] is an evidence of a life-changing encounter with Jesus. It does not imply sinlessness!"[324] "The ones who persevere are the same ones who are saved."[325] True believers "are kept by the power of God through faith unto salvation" (1 Peter 1:5). Eternal security of the believer is a bedrock of the Christian faith. See John 6:37. William MacDonald comments, "Although saving faith may have lapses, it always has the quality of permanence."[326] Leon Morris adds, "The power of God is such that He can and will sustain His faithful servants through whatever trials they may be called upon to endure."[327]

How long must the believer persevere in trials? "To the end." Morris says, "'To the end' means not only to the end of some period of time, but to the end of the trials, the persecutions. It is not good enough for the follower of Jesus to renounce his allegiance somewhere along the line. Real discipleship means perseverance right through whatever trials the world throws in our way."[328] And such trials will only cease upon the believer's exodus to Heaven. Spurgeon remarked, "To forsake the Lord through persecution is to set time before eternity, to barter Heaven for this world's pleasures, to renounce eternal life for a few hours of ease, and to involve ourselves in endless misery rather than endure a stupid jest or a senseless jibe. It comes to that. Like true soldiers may we buckle on our harness and resolve that, let the battle rage as it may, through divine grace we will not desert our colors. We prefer death itself to the disgrace of forsaking a cause so true, a doctrine so pure, a Savior so gracious, a Prince so noble and so worthy of our most loyal service."[329] And to that, I say a hearty, Amen.

The psalmist battling numerous mighty and able foes said, "*I had fainted*, unless I had believed to see the goodness of the LORD in the land of the living" (Psalm 27:13). That which kept David from 'fainting' was unshakeable faith (wholehearted trust, full confidence) in God that He would sustain him in the midst of the grievous trial. This assurance stemmed from David's intimate knowledge of and walk with God and His sacred promises. Whereas there are numerous helps to enable the saint's endurance in persecution, ultimately, this is the pivotal one.

> Faint not, Christian! tho' the road
> Leading to thy blest abode
> Darksome be and dangerous too—
> Christ, thy Guide, will bring thee thro'.

> Faint not, Christian! tho' the world
> Hath its hostile flag unfurled.
> Hold the cross of Jesus fast;
> Thou shalt overcome at last.

Faint not, Christian! Though in rage
Satan doth thy soul engage.
Take thee faith's anointed shield;
Bear it to the battlefield.

Faint not, Christian! Christ is near;
Soon in glory He'll appear.
Then shall end thy toil and strife,
Death be swallowed up of life.

~ J. H. Evans (1866)

Winston Churchill offers the persecuted some grave encouragement: "Never give in. Never give in. Never, never, never, never—in nothing, great or small, large or petty—never give in, except to convictions of honor and good sense. Never yield to force. Never yield to the apparently overwhelming might of the enemy."[330] In the face of hostile oppression for the faith, the devoted believer says with Nehemiah as he battled the same, "I'm not the kind of person that runs and hides" (Nehemiah 6:11 GNT).

24
Cautionary Counsel

"For so did they persecute." This was expressly added, that the apostles might not expect to triumph without exertion and without a contest, and might not fail when they encountered persecutions."[331]

~ John Calvin

"For so did they persecute the prophets" (Matthew 5:12 ANT). That is, if godly men of old encountered grievous persecution for the faith, then they (apostles and all believers) would likewise. The prophets, who are likened unto the apostles in status (frontline warriors pushing back darkness), serve as examples of the hostility (persecution) believers will encounter and have to endure in proclaiming the truth. The warning was well justified, for the disciples envisioned Christ's kingdom to be a type of utopia on earth, certainly not one of conflict.

It is expedient that believers heed the same cautionary counsel and awaken to the consciousness that persecution will come (primarily to the spiritual, not the carnal; contrast the Smyrna saints [Revelation 2:8–10] with the Laodicean saints [Revelation 3:14–18]). As John R. Rice says, "The world never burned a casual Christian at the stake."[332] Avoid the trap of thinking that somehow, unlike the prophets of old, you will escape persecution for Christ's name's sake (something which is impossible for the godly—2 Timothy 3:12).

Thomas à Kempis observed 600 years ago, "The devil sleepeth not, neither is the flesh as yet dead; therefore, cease not to prepare thyself for the battle, for on thy right hand and on thy left are enemies who never rest." And he is still right. Suddenly and unexpectedly hostile forces today may attack your Christian faith, convictions, values, and religious freedom at the workplace, mission post, schoolhouse, church house, and your house. Stay ready to stand firm in your resistance in its wake. George Whitefield remarked, "If we would therefore behave like good soldiers of Jesus Christ, we must be always on our guard and never pretend to lay down our spiritual weapons of prayer and watching till our warfare is ended by death; for if we do, our spiritual foe will quickly prevail against us."[333] See 2 Timothy 2:3–4. Keep the sabre ready (Ephesians 6:17).

25
Promise of Present Blessedness
"Persecutions are pledges of God's love, badges of honor."[334]
~ Thomas Watson

He that is persecuted for Christ's sake (having evil spoken about them falsely and experiencing outward forms of hostile violence, Matthew 5:10–11[335]) will be "blessed" presently (incomprehensible happiness and the deepest inner joy[336]) by Christ's personal touch. The promise is a grace-gift bestowed by Christ (not a debt paid as remuneration for the persecution), a point Weber makes in saying, "Kingdom honor is not granted as compensation for the unfairness of life, but as a blessing on those who have actively pursued true kingdom righteousness and have been persecuted for it."[337] The promise (blessedness) is not based upon the scope of the persecution (size or form) but upon the patient endurance of it (1 Peter 2:20b). And its measure (degree of blessedness) is determined by the amount of suffering incurred for Christ.[338] What a glorious and uplifting promise! (For the promised future reward in Heaven [Matthew 5:12], see Chapter 11, *The Crown of Life*).

But it has exceptions, as does the reward to be given in Heaven. It is not for all the persecuted, but only for those persecuted for the sake of Christ. John Wesley said, "If we suffer persecution and affliction in a right manner, we attain a larger measure of conformity to Christ, by a due improvement of one of these occasions, than we could have done merely by imitating his mercy in abundance of good works."[339] "Lest thou shouldest think," said Chrysostom, "that the mere fact of being evil spoken of makes men blessed, He has set two limitations: when it is for His sake and when the things that are said are false, for without these he who is evil spoken of, so far from being blessed, is miserable."[340] Leon Morris states, "Believers are not to engage in the kind of conduct [unethical, immoral, dishonest] that enables people to accuse them genuinely; their lives are to be above reproach."[341]

The promise also excludes believers that seek persecution for notoriety or personal gain, or who are just plain obnoxious. Oswald Chambers states, "Many of us awaken antagonism by our way of stating things; we have to distinguish between being persecuted for some notion of our own and being persecuted 'for My sake.'"[342] Jon Courson says, "Many times Christians are being persecuted not because they're living righteously, but because they're weird. Weirdness doesn't count!"[343] "Christians are often persecuted," states Ken Hughes, "not for their Christianity, but for their lack of it. Sometimes they simply have unpleasant personalities. They are rude, insensitive, thoughtless—piously obnoxious. Some are rejected because they are discerned as proud and judgmental. Others are disliked because they are lazy and irresponsible. Either arrogance or incompetence mixed with piety is sure to bring rejection."[344] Saith Alan Redpath, "It is perfectly possible for a Christian to be so aggressive and objectionable in his witness that he brings suffering on himself. Though he may say it's the price of being true to the Lord, the fact is he deserves all he gets. To be sound in doctrine but sullen in temper, to be Christlike in creed but critical in tongue, to be faithful in church work at the expense of duty to home is to invite well deserved and scathing comment of everybody."[345]

> Take care that your cross is indeed the cross of Christ. If it be brought upon you by your own fault or imprudence, it is your own cross, and not the cross of Christ.
> Charles Simeon

Charles Simeon cautions, "Take care that your cross is indeed the cross of Christ. If it be brought upon you by your own fault or imprudence, it is your own cross, and not the cross of Christ. See that you do not, from a pretended zeal for God, neglect or violate your duties to man. If you suffer, take care that it is for well-doing and not for evil doing."[346]

26
Inspirational Sayings of Saints

"The ear of the wise listens to instruction, and the heart of the wise discerns what is heard to acquire knowledge."[347]
~ Allen Ross

"If you have knowledge," says Thomas Fuller, "let others light their candles at it."[348] Lower your "candle" to the flames of the following saints to have it ignited with their wise counsel and encouragement regarding persecution and suffering.

Horatius Bonar

"Someone, then, must undertake the ungracious task of probing and laying bare the evils of the age, for men must not be allowed to congratulate themselves that all is well. If others will not, he will. If others shrink from the obloquy of such a work, he will not. He loves the age too well; he loves his nation too well; he loves his fellowmen too well. They may upbraid him; they may call him a misanthropist or a prophet of evil; they may ascribe his warnings to the worst of motives, such as pride or arrogance or self-esteem or malice or envy; but he will give no heed to these unjust insinuations. He will prefer being thus misunderstood and maligned to allowing men to precipitate themselves upon a ruin which they see not. Rather than that they should perish, he will allow his own good name to be spoken against. He will risk everything, even the hatred of brethren, rather than withhold the warning."

Leonard Ravenhill

"We raise our hats to the martyrs, and we thank God for the last drop of their blood, but we won't give Him the first drop of ours. If you stir Hell up, the Devil will stir everything he can against you: you'll get misunderstood, misrepresented....[I]f you're not mature enough, it will get you down. It's not the contradiction of sinners,...[i]t's the criticism of saints that gets you down."[349]

George Horne

"Slander and calumny must always precede and accompany persecution, because malice itself cannot excite people against a good man, as such; to do this, he must first be represented as a bad man. What can be said of those who are busied in this manner but that they are a 'generation of vipers,' the brood of the old 'Serpent,' that grand accuser and calumniator of the brethren, having under their tongues a bag of 'poison' conveying instant death to the reputation on which they fasten. Thus, David was hunted as a rebel, Christ was crucified as a blasphemer, and the primitive Christians were tortured as guilty."

G. K. Chesterton

"Tolerance is the virtue of a man without convictions."[350]

R. G. Lee

In describing Paul, Dr. R. G. Lee said, "Self-sacrifice was his life's law; Calvary was his life's passion. Paul was as courageous as he was faithful. Paul was as indifferent to criticism as he was stubborn for righteousness."[351]

Henry Ward Beecher

"There are a hundred men hacking at the branches of evil to every one who is striking at the roots of evil."[352]

A. W. Tozer

"I have the right to disappoint men in order to avoid disappointing God."[353] "The idea that this world is a playground instead of a battleground has now been accepted in practice by the vast majority of fundamentalist Christians."[354]

Thomas Watson

"No sooner is any man a minister, but he is part martyr. The ministers of Christ are His chosen vessels. Now as the best vessel of gold and silver passes through the fire, so God's chosen vessels pass often through the fire of persecution. Ministers must expect an alarm."[355]

George W. Truett

"Persecution may make men hypocrites, but it will not make them Christians."[356]

John of Kronstadt

"Do not be despondent when fighting against the incorporeal enemy, but even in the midst of your afflictions and oppression praise the Lord who has found you worthy to suffer for Him by struggling against the subtlety of the serpent, and to be wounded for Him at every hour; for had you not lived piously and endeavored to become united to God, the enemy would not have attacked and tormented you."[357]

Robert M. M'Cheyne

"Do not forget the culture of the inner man—I mean of the heart. How diligently the cavalry officer keeps his saber clean and sharp; every stain he rubs off with the greatest care. Remember you are God's sword, His instrument. In great measure, according to the purity and perfections of the instrument will be the success. It is not great talents God blesses so much as a great likeness to Jesus. A holy minister is an awful weapon in the hand of God."[358]

Martin Luther

"I have held many things in my hands, and I have lost them all; but whatever I have placed in God's hands, that I still possess."[359]

Matthew Henry

"Whatever is the object for which men forsake Christ, that is the price at which Satan buys their souls."[360]

Justin Martyr

"You can kill us, but you cannot hurt us."[361] In the year 165 he was beheaded for the faith.

C. H. Spurgeon

"The art of persecuting has been so long studied by the seed of the serpent that they are perfect masters of it and know how to make the iron enter into the soul. Do not be astonished, therefore, if you are sorely vexed; neither be amazed, as though some strange thing hdd happened unto you. The martyrs did not suffer sham pains; the racks on which they were stretched were not beds of ease, nor were their prisons parlors of comfort. Their pains were agonies; their martyrdoms were torments. If you had sham griefs, you might expect counterfeit joys; let the reality of your tribulation assure you of the reality of the coming glory."[362]

"The persecuted saint occupies a place where he warns and enlightens, and therefore suffers. He is like an advanced guard to whom the place of danger is the place of honor; only let him ask for strength to bear and forbear, and he shall have glory at the last."[363]

William Gurnall

"And while God had work for Paul, he found him friends both in court and prison. Let persecutors send saints to prison; God can provide a keeper for their turn."[364]

D. L. Moody

"I'm so thankful that I have a joy that the world cannot rob me of; I have a treasure that the world cannot take from me; I have something that is not in the power of man or devil to deprive me of, and that is the joy of the Lord. 'No man taketh it from you.' In the second century, they brought a martyr before a king, and the king wanted him to recant and give up Christ and Christianity, but the man spurned the proposition. But the king said, 'If you don't do it, I will banish you.' The man smiled and answered, 'You can't banish me from Christ, for He says He will never leave me nor forsake me.' The king got angry and said, 'Well, I will confiscate your property and take it all from you.' And the man replied, 'My treasures are laid up on high; you cannot get them.' The king became still more angry and said, 'I will kill you.' 'Why,' the man answered, 'I have been dead forty years; I have been dead with Christ, dead to the world, and my life is hid with Christ in God, and you cannot touch it.' And so we can rejoice, because we are on resurrection ground, having risen with Christ. Let persecution and opposition come, we can rejoice continually and remember that our reward is great, reserved for us unto the day when He who is our Life shall appear and we shall appear with Him in glory."

Henry Smith

"God examineth with trials; the Devil examineth with temptations; the world examineth with persecutions."[365]

J. I. Packer

"We think less and less about the better things that Christ will bring us at His reappearance because our thoughts are increasingly absorbed by the good things we enjoy here. No one would wish persecution or destitution on another, but who can deny that at this point they might do us good?"[366]

Martin Luther

"If I profess with the loudest voice and clearest exposition every portion of the truth of God except precisely that little point which the world and the Devil are at the moment attacking, I am not confessing Christ, however boldly I may be professing Christ. Where the battle rages, there the loyalty of the soldier is proved. And to be steady on all the battle fields besides is merely flight and disgrace if he flinches at that point."[367]

J. C. Ryle

"Let it be a settled principle in our minds, that the true Christian must always enter the kingdom of God 'through much tribulation' (Acts 14:22). If we are faithful and decided servants of Christ, the world will certainly hate us, as it hated our Master. In one way or another, true grace will always be persecuted. No consistency of conduct, however faultless; no kindness and amiability of character, however striking, will exempt a believer from the world's dislike so long as he lives. It is foolish to be surprised at this. It is part of the cross, and we must bear it patiently."[368]

Cyprian of Carthage

"It is a bad world, Donatus, an incredibly bad world. But I have discovered in the midst of it a quiet and good people who have learned the great secret of life. They have found a joy and wisdom which is a thousand times better than any of the pleasures of our sinful life. They are despised and persecuted, but they care not. They are masters of their souls. They have overcome the world. These people, Donatus, are Christians…and I am one of them."[369]

Charles Simeon

"God does not 'send you on a warfare at your own charges.' He bids you to 'commit your soul to him in well-doing,' with an assured hope that He will keep it. Your merciful Savior, who has trod the way before you, will sympathize with you under your trials and overrule them all for good, and in due time put you safely, and forever, beyond the reach of all."[370]

Charles Finney

"The restraints of public opinion change the form of persecution, yet by no means expel its spirit. Enmity against God is the spirit of murder against God's people. Persecution driven from one form flies to another. Driven from the civil sword, it flies to ecclesiastical fulminations. Persecutors always justify themselves by misrepresenting and calumniating the men they would persecute. They maligned the ancient prophets thus as enemies of the State, Christ as a blasphemer, the apostles as those who had turned the world upside down. So it will ever be. Very few indeed will allow themselves to believe that they are persecuting men for their righteousness' sake. But they do allow themselves to be deceived. Nay they may unconsciously court deception. In our own times men allow themselves to jeer and taunt religious men and religion itself, as if this were not persecution. They allow themselves to be deceived in regard to the character of those whom they persecute.

They would be shocked if told, "You persecute Christ in his people." So they first make it appear that Christ is not in such people and then give loose to their malignity."[371]

Billy Graham

"Since we have experienced little religious persecution in this country, it is likely that under pressure many would deny Christ. Those who shout the loudest about their faith may surrender soonest. Many who boast of being courageous would be cowardly. Many who say, 'Though all others deny Christ, yet I will never deny Him,' would be the first to warm their hands at the campfires of the enemy. Jesus, in speaking of the last times, warned, 'Then they will deliver you up to tribulation and kill you, and you will be hated by all nations for My name's sake' (Matthew 24:9 NKJV). The Scripture says, 'Because lawlessness will abound, the love of many will grow cold' (Matthew 24:12 NKJV). The Apostle Paul, referring to the coming evil day, said, 'Therefore take up the whole armor of God, that you may be able to withstand in the evil day, and having done all, to stand' (Ephesians 6:13 NKJV)."[372]

John Foxe

"Which prophecy of Christ we see wonderfully to be verified, insomuch that the whole course of the Church to this day may seem nothing else but a verifying of the said prophecy. First, that Christ hath set up a Church needeth no declaration. Second, what force of princes, kings, monarchs, governors, and rulers of this world, with their subjects, publicly and privately, with all their strength and cunning have bent themselves against this Church! And, third, how the said Church, all this notwithstanding hath yet endured and holden its own!"[373]

John Gill

"Knowing that they [disciples] had all imbibed the same notion of a temporal kingdom and were in expectation of worldly riches, honor, and pleasure, Jesus took this opportunity of preaching the doctrine of the cross to them [Matthew 16:24], and of letting them know that they must prepare for persecutions, sufferings, and death, which they must expect to endure as well as He, if they would be His disciples."[374]

David Brainerd

"I cared not how I lived or what hardships I might go through so that I could gain souls for Christ. While I was asleep, I dreamed of these things; and when I awaked, the first thing I thought of was this great work."[375]

Jonathan Edwards

"True virtue never appears so lovely as when it is most oppressed, and the divine excellency of real Christianity is never exhibited with such advantage as when under the greatest trials; then it is that true faith appears much more precious than gold!"[376]

Dietrich Bonhoeffer

"The messengers of Jesus will be hated to the end of time. They will be blamed for all the division which rend cities and homes. Jesus and His disciples will be condemned on all sides for undermining family life and for leading the nation astray; they will be called crazy fanatics and disturbers of the peace. The disciples will be sorely tempted to desert their Lord. But the end is also near, and they must hold on and persevere until it comes. Only he will be blessed who remains loyal to Jesus and His Word until the end."[377]

27
Persecution and Eschatological Prophecy

Friend, you are living in the beginning of the end. The end of the world is near!"[378]

~ *Larry Poland*

With the disciples, all believers are exhorted to analyze the eschatological signs of the end time in order to identify it when it arrives (Luke 21:29–31). But most do not. And for this Christ gives reprimand. He said that observation of a cloud rising in the west prompts belief that it soon will rain, and rain it does (Luke 12:54). Also, when it is noted that the south wind is blowing, it is said it will be a hot day. And a scorcher it is (Luke 12:55). And then He said, "You know how to analyze the appearance of the earth and the sky, but why do you not analyze this present time?" (Luke 12:56 NASB). Biblical analysis of the "present time" certainly parallels with Jesus' prophecy of the end time (what it will be like in the last days is a photograph of the present time). The signs of the end time include that of widespread persecution and oppression of the saints (Matthew 24:3–12). David Jeremiah says, "The more the Gospel progresses and the closer we come to the end of the age, the more aggressive the enemy becomes."[379]

David Limbaugh writes, "Anti-Christian discrimination in our society is getting more blatant and widespread every day. The cultural assumptions of our society influence changes in the law, and the culture is moving against the public expression of Christian belief."[380] The intensification and worsening of Christian *persecution* signals (or is a signpost of) the return of Christ to judge the wicked and set up His millennial kingdom.[381] With regard to the "last days" (the period between Christ's resurrection and His return), Jesus said, "Then you will be arrested, persecuted, and killed. You will be hated all over the world because you are my followers. And many will turn away from me and betray and hate each other" (Matthew 24:9–10 NLT). These end-time prophecies along with others, including that which Paul states in 2 Timothy 3:1–5 (19 signs of end-time corruption and lawlessness), certainly indicate that we are living in the "days of Noah" (Matthew 24:37). With regard to these "last days" indicators (prophecies), Jesus said, "And when these things begin to come to pass, then look up, and lift up your heads; for your redemption draweth nigh" (Luke 21:28).

Hal Lindsey, in his book *Planet Earth—2000 A.D.*, states that persecution will only escalate and intensify; but before it becomes "unbearable," Christ will return for His people.[382] Alan Redpath says, "There is no member of His body who is exempt from bearing his quota of suffering for His absent Lord, and as this age comes to its great climax and Satan has his final fling, it is to be expected, and indeed it is clearly stated in the Word of God, that the path of the true Christian will become more and more difficult."[383]

The "labor pains" of persecution are visible, widespread, and being exacerbated. "Over the decade from 2007 to 2017, government restrictions on religion—laws, policies and actions by state officials that restrict religious beliefs and practices—increased markedly around the world,"[384] stated the [Pew] researchers. And social hostilities involving religion—including violence and harassment by private individuals, organizations or groups—also have risen since 2007."[385] Three hundred million Christians around the world suffer persecution. One of seven believers live in countries where they are persecuted. In 2014 Christians suffered persecution in 108 countries. In 2015 the number increased to 128 countries, and in 2018 it jumped to 143 countries. Radical extremist Islam is responsible for the suffering of believers in 22 of the worst-persecuting countries. Eleven Christians are killed every single day in the severest persecuting countries of the world.[386] In the past 100 years, more Christians have died on behalf of Christ than in all prior centuries combined since Jesus' time.[387] Though impossible to know, researchers report that 90,000 or more believers were killed in 2016 "for Christ's sake" alone.[388]

Speaking at the State Department's second Ministerial to Advance Religious Freedom in Washington, Rep. Chris Smith, R-New Jersey, said, "The terrible, largely unacknowledged reality is this: We are witnessing in the early 21st century an international megacrisis in religious freedom. Religious persecution is festering and exploding around the world."[389] The world of faith is under siege," he said. "We are at a tipping point—threats are multiplying by the day." The acceleration and expansion of persecution throughout the world (the siege of evil through censorship, discrimination, retaliation, and infliction of pain and suffering on Christians) clearly is a "signpost" indicating that we are living in the *last of the last days* that point to the return of Christ (Matthew 24:44). "Let your moderation be known unto all men. The Lord is at hand [the Lord is coming soon]" (Philippians 4:5), and, "Wherefore comfort one another with these words" (I Thessalonians 4:18).

28
Ministry to the Persecuted Church

"While Christians in America have worshipped without the fear or threat of physical abuse for their beliefs, thousands of their brothers in Christ throughout the world have been tortured and martyred for confessing the name of Christ."[390]

~ Billy Graham

Presently 245 million believers globally encounter intimidation, affliction or prison for the cause of Christ, with the worst cases being in Iraq (ISIS), the Middle East (Al-Qaeda), North Korea (Kim Jong-un), India (Hindu nationalists), Somalia and Kenya (Al-Shabaab), Northern Nigeria (Boko Haram), Northern Nigeria Middle Belt (militant Fulani herdsmen), Asia: Bangladesh, Indonesia; and Africa: Egypt, Nigeria, Somalia (radical Islam), Colombia and Mexico (drug cartels), and China (the Chinese Communist Party).[391] These are but a sampling; many more easily could be added to the list. (The freest of the big countries for religious liberty are South Africa, Japan, the Philippines, Brazil, and South Korea. The United States falls in the center of the grouping.[392])

The saint must exhibit concern for the persecuted church around the world. Thomas Schirrmacher, in his book *The Persecution of Christians Concerns Us All,* says that "committed efforts to aid persecuted Christians cannot be left up to a few enthusiasts but, according the New Testament, is a central duty of the Christian church."[393] All that live godly lives will be persecuted in some form and measure (2 Timothy 3:12), many more severely than others. Christians that are persecuted "less" severely (mildly, by contrast) must seek to help those that experience extreme and violent oppression. He that has a "voice" must speak up for him that does not.

The writer of Hebrews admonishes, "Remember them that are in bonds, as bound with them; and them which suffer adversity, as being yourselves also in the body" (Hebrews 13:3). How is it that we are to treat fellow believers in persecution?

(1. **With contemplation.** "Remember them." The implication is that saints are prone to forget those who are persecuted (imprisoned and oppressed) for Christ's sake. To remember is "to remind oneself" or intentionally recall the estate of the persecuted one and "as a result, respond in an appropriate manner."[394] It means "to give careful consideration to, think of, care for, be concerned about, keep in mind."[395] It is not to be a passive remembrance. Mere remembrance without action is futile. Most Christians are asleep in ignorance or sinful unconcern regarding to the perilous plight of millions of believers suffering atrocious persecution for the sake of Christ and must be awakened to rally to their support.

(2. **With identification.** "As bound with them"; that is, as shackled to them bearing the same affliction. Be identical to them;[396] put yourself in their shoes. See Hebrews 10:34. Douglas Bazi, a minister in Northern Iraq, said, "Suffering is not killing us, but to suffer alone is killing us."[397] Brothers and sisters in the furnace of affliction for Christ's sake must know that they are not forgotten; they do not stand alone in their resistance to hostile forces of the faith.

(3. **With obligation.** As being them ("yourselves also in the body"). "Bear ye one another's burdens" (Galatians 6:2). How? By exhibiting hearty sympathy for them. Paul admonishes, "Weep with them that weep" (Romans 12:15). Burke says, "Sympathy may be considered as a sort of substitution, by which we are put into the place of another man and affected in many respects as he is affected."[398] First, sympathize heartily with the persecuted, as you would want others to do for you in the similar circumstance (what others suffer for Christ's sake, you likewise may suffer). It is said of Origen, "Not only was he at the side of the holy martyrs in their imprisonment and until their final condemnation, but when they were led to death, he boldly accompanied them into danger."[399]

Richard Wurmbrand, an evangelical minister who endured 14 years of Communist imprisonment and torture in his homeland of Romania, was such a sympathizer. He wrote, "I tremble because of the sufferings of those persecuted in different lands. I tremble thinking about the eternal destiny of their torturers. I tremble for

Western Christians who don't help their persecuted brethren. In the depth of my heart, I would like to keep the beauty of my own vineyard and not be involved in such a huge fight. I would like so much to be somewhere in quietness and rest. But it is not possible.... The quietness and rest for which I long would be an escape from reality and dangerous for my soul....The West sleeps and *must be awakened to see the plight* of the captive nations."[400] This book, in part, is purposed to bring about that awakening.

Second, we help bear the burden of the oppressed through relieving or lessening their pain, discomfort and need. Tertullian, in the third century, writes in *The Apology,* "If there happens to be any in the mines or banished to the islands or shut up in prisons for nothing but their fidelity to the cause of God's church, they become the nurslings of the Christians." In other words, it's the Christian's responsibility to render whatever help is needed to our persecuted brethren.

Be more than a "companion" to them that suffer. The Hebrews writer beckons, "But call to remembrance the former days, in which, after ye were illuminated, ye endured a great fight of afflictions; Partly, whilst ye were made a gazingstock both by reproaches and afflictions; and partly, whilst ye became companions of them that were so used" (Hebrews 10:32–33).

Though some Christians were made a public spectacle ("gazingstock") in their persecution (scourging, tormenting, execution) in amphitheaters (to fight beasts), courts of justice, and theatrical stages, others escaped. See I Corinthians 4:9 and I Corinthians 15:32. Of the latter, the Bible says they "became *companions* (more than mere companionship;[401] a joint-participator[402]) of them that were so used (maltreated, tormented, executed)". That is, these early believers sympathized and identified with those that suffered for "Christ's sake" and doubtlessly rendered monetary and/or other forms of relief from their personal belongings. Matthew Poole comments, "They were consorts and sharers of all those members of Christ who were so abused by the devil and his instruments, and they bore their burdens with them, were inwardly grieved for them, publicly owned and comforted them, supplied and supported them as they could."[403]

Instances are recorded of the early saints not only raising money for the release of the persecuted but actually selling themselves into slavery for that purpose.[404] Aristides of Athens said of the early Christians, "If they hear that any one of their number is imprisoned or in distress for the sake of their Christ's name, they all render aid in his necessity, and if he can be redeemed, they set him free."[405] Christian's ought to likewise impart such sympathy and support to their brothers and sisters persecuted today. See Hebrews 10:34. In fact, it is the Christian's duty to rescue saints who for "Christ's sake" are unjustly being executed (martyred) and those whose lives stand in deadly peril for the same. Queen Esther, at risk to her own life, intervened in behalf of the Jews (Esther 4:16). Reuben rescued Joseph from death (Genesis 37:20–22). Jonathan saved David from the sword of King Saul (1 Samuel 19:1–6). Ebed-melech and Ahikam rescued Jeremiah from the deep miry pit of death (Jeremiah 26:24; 38:11–13). Paul's sister's son saved Paul's life in telling the Roman chief captain of a murderous plot to kill him (Acts 23:16–22). These rescuers kept back them "that are drawn unto death, and those that are ready to be slain" (Proverbs 24:11) at risk of personal peril. With information abundantly available about the persecution of believers globally, we cannot pretend ignorance, "We knew it not" (Proverbs 24:12), with regard to their dire estate and need of help.

Practical ways to make *provision* for the persecuted.

(1. Contribute to their legal defense cost.

(2. Supply funding for food, clothing and shelter.

(3. Be an advocate for those who are imprisoned or facing a death sentence by intervening with the government.

(4. Communicate with them by letters or emails of encouragement and hope, providing their safety is not thereby endangered.

(5. Provide a hiding place of refuge for them, as Rahab did for the two spies (Joshua 2:3–4) and Corrie ten Boom *(The Hiding Place)* did for the Jews.

(6. Adopt a persecuted church people group as a church family to whom to minister (mission trips, budget support, etc., wherever it is possible).

(7. Personally visit the persecuted to provide assistance on the ground, if you can do so without serious endangerment to them or yourself. "Boots on the ground" in any battle are extremely beneficial.

(8. Sow and cultivate the message of religious liberty as the innate right of all men.

(9. Increase awareness among all saints of the dire estate of their persecuted brothers and sisters, and rally them to their support.

(10. Dispense needed biblical literature (Bibles, tracts, Sunday school lessons, etc.).

Third, the believer eases the burden of the persecuted through various means of encouragement (Philippians 4:18). In Corinth, experiencing extreme trouble, torment and trial (Acts 18:5–17; 1 Corinthians 2:3), Paul reached a point that he couldn't 'bear it any longer' (1 Thessalonians 3:5). Upon word of the Thessalonican saints' steadfastness in the faith, their longing to see him, and their love (all shared by Timothy), Paul's distraught spirit was infused with renewed vigor, his diminished strength was revived (1 Thessalonians 3:6–8) and his decreased spriteliness refreshed (1 Thessalonians 3:9). Let us not devalue the power of communicating the same to the persecuted to enliven, encourage and energize.

Fourth, and most importantly, we assist the persecuted with their burden by providing prayer *for* them (Romans 15:30–31; Philippians 1:19, 22) and provision *to* them (Philippians 4:10).

Father of mercies! send Thy grace
    All-powerful from above,
To form in our obedient souls
    The image of Thy love.

Oh, may our sympathizing breasts
    The generous pleasure know,
Kindly to share in others' joy
    And weep for others' woe!

When the most helpless sons of grief
In low distress are laid,
Soft be our hearts their pains to feel
And swift our hands to aid.

~ Philip Doddridge (1702–1751)

Paul Chitwood, International Mission Board President of the Southern Baptist Convention, said, "Prayer is our greatest resource in the Great Commission, and it is also the greatest act of compassion we could perform for our brothers and sisters around the globe who are enduring persecution. Just as the souls of those slain for their faith cry out in Heaven, 'O Sovereign Lord, holy and true, how long before you will judge and avenge our blood' (Revelation 6:10 ESV), we should cry out on behalf of those on earth who continue to suffer. We ask God to give them courage and hope. We know that their temporary suffering will be rewarded in eternity and pray that it will result in many being saved from among the nations."[406] The first Sunday in June annually is designated by the SBC as a Day of Prayer for the Persecuted Church. See 2 Corinthians 1:11.

John Calvin states, "Against the persecution of a tyrant the godly have no remedy but prayer."[407] Brother Andrew (God's Smuggler) said, "Through prayer, we have the ability to move beyond borders and into the very presence of our enemies."[408]

> Against the persecution of a tyrant the godly have no remedy but prayer.
> John Calvin

Practical ways to *pray* for the persecuted.

(1. Pray for access to the Bible. Many live in *Bible deserts.*

(2. Pray for safety from persecutors. Pray the psalmist prayer in their behalf, "My times are in your hand; rescue me from the hand of my enemies and from my persecutors!" (Psalm 31:15 ESV).

(3. Pray for courage like a lion in facing opposition and persecution and prosecution (imprisonment, execution, torture). A

Chinese missionary said, "The prayer of Chinese believers is not that the persecution would stop, but that they would have the strength to remain faithful."[409]

(4. Pray for secrecy of their hiding places from the hostile.

(5. Pray that they may remain in their homeland messaging the Gospel.

(6. Pray for Holy Spirit discernment to govern their conduct, conversation and confrontations, and His empowerment to enable their ministry and perseverance.

(7. Pray that the God of all comfort will grant consolation, calm and encouragement.

(8. Pray that the material losses (home, land, possessions, money, stock animals, etc.) incurred for "Christ's sake" will be restored and/or be provided by their brothers and sisters in the faith around the world.

(9. Pray that the cost of litigation (court, lawyer) to secure their vindication and/or freedom from imprisonment be supplied.

(10. Pray that those who are rejected and abandoned by family and friends will be united with other believers by God.

(11. Pray for the ruler and decision makers in their land. Jerry Bridges comments, "Prayer is the most tangible expression of trust in God. If we would trust God for our persecuted brothers and sisters in other countries, we must be diligent in prayer for their rulers. If we would trust God when decisions of government in our own country go against our best interests, we must pray for His working in the hearts of those officials and legislators who make those decisions. The truth that the king's heart is in the hand of the Lord is meant to be a stimulus to prayer, not a stimulus to a fatalistic attitude."[410] See Proverbs 21:1. William Tyndale prayed, "Lord, open the King of England's eyes."[411]

(12. Pray that their worship and Bible teaching be unhindered.

(13. Pray that God will use their witness to ignite a flame for righteousness, religious liberty, and His cause, that neither Satan nor man may extinguish.

(14. Pray for open doors to evangelize.

(15. Pray that by some means they will know you are interceding in their behalf (2 Timothy 1:3).

(16. Pray that they might be filled with divine wisdom, discernment and illumination.

(17. Pray they will have grace to forgive their persecutor(s).

We pray for saints we know not,
    For saints still yet to be,
For grace to bear true witness
    And serve You faithfully.

~ Horatio Nelson (1864)

In addition to praying practically in the ways mentioned, pray specifically for the needs of persecuted saints and churches as shared by mission organizations and advocates for the persecuted church in the world. Be an agonizing prayer warrior for the persecuted as Epaphras was (Colossians 4:12–13).

> To enhance your consistent praying for the persecuted church in the aforementioned ways, set your watch or cell phone alarm to ring at 13:03 daily (military time for 1:03 p.m.).

Hebrews 13:3 challenges us to "remember them that are in bonds." To enhance your consistent praying for the persecuted church in the aforementioned ways, set your watch or cell phone alarm to ring at 13:03 daily (military time for 1:03 p.m.). Even the simplest and shortest of prayers are of immense benefit to the persecuted.

Faith of our brothers, suffering sore,
    Enduring prison, famine, and sword,
O Holy Spirit, give comfort, we pray;
    May they this day find strength in Thy Word.
Faith of our brothers, holy faith,
May they be true to thee till death!

Tortured and killed for Thy dear name,
    Lord, give them grace to count all but loss;
May they hold steadfast to the end,
    Sharing the sufferings of the cross.
Faith of our brothers, holy faith,
May they be true to thee till death!

Our brothers, chained in prisons dark,
    Are still in heart and conscience free.
Oh, may they know thy deep, sweet peace;
    Fill them with joy for all to see.
Faith of our brothers, holy faith,
May they be true to thee till death!

Faith of our brothers! May they love
    Both friend and foe in all their strife
And preach Thee too as love knows how
    By kindly words and virtuous life.
Faith of our brothers, holy faith,
May they be true to thee till death!

And, Lord, may we be ready too
    To give our lives, if needed, for Thee;
May we be strong in Thy great strength
    And live each day committed to Thee.
Faith of all brothers, holy faith,
May we be true to thee till death!
                    ~ Adapted by Susan H. Peterson (1997)

Three men risked their lives to get David water from the well
near the gate of Bethlehem that was guarded by Philistine soldiers
(2 Samuel 23:16). But David refused to drink it. The water having
been attained at far too great a cost, the jeopardy of the men's
lives, he poured the water onto the ground as an offering unto God.
I feel the same as David with regard to the millions of persecuted
and martyred saints who jeopardized and are jeopardizing even
life itself to secure the "water" which all of Christendom enjoys
today. With Paul I say to them and the entire persecuted church of

yesterday, today and tomorrow, "We can't help but thank God for you, because your faith is flourishing and your love for one another is growing. We proudly tell God's other churches about your endurance and faithfulness in all the persecutions and hardships you are suffering. And God will use this persecution to show his justice and to make you worthy of his Kingdom, for which you are suffering. In his justice he will pay back those who persecute you. And God will provide rest for you who are being persecuted and also for us when the Lord Jesus appears from heaven" (2 Thessalonians 1:3–7 NLT).

H. M. Butler well says, "These heroes of all time, these the salt of the world who saved it from utter corruption and by the very blood which their persecutors poured out sowed the seed which was to renew the face of the earth, these [are] representatives of what man can be when he allows God to work in him mightily."[412] By their suffering and sacrifice, doors that were shut to the Gospel opened; the blessed Bible, though ridiculed and burned, was preserved without error; heresy was exposed and truth magnified; religious liberty and freedom of speech were attained; evil and wicked tyrants were disposed and myriads of people converted. All this we receive as a gift from their hands—as the blood of men who jeopardized and sacrificed their lives for the cause of Christ and His glory and my best good. Let us, with David, take what they have done and pour it out unto God as an offering of thanksgiving in their honor.[413] God forbid that we forget the price that has been paid and is being paid by persecuted saints to propagate the Gospel and acquire religious freedom around the world. Therefore, the Bible says, 'Remember them,' and 'Relieve them,' and if necessary, 'Rescue them.' And when called upon, "Resemble them" (suffer as them).

> By all Your saints still striving,
>   For all Your saints at rest,
> Your holy name, O Jesus,
>   Forevermore be blessed!

For those passed on before us,
We sing our praise anew
And, walking in their footsteps,
Would live our lives for You.

~ Horatio Nelson (1864)

Visit the website for *Open Doors USA* (www.opendoorsusa. org/resources) for assistance in rendering aid to the persecuted church, and https://billygraham.org/video/persecution-and-the-gospel/ to view *Persecution and the Gospel*, a documentary on the wide-spread Christian persecution in the world.

29
Of Whom the World Is Not Worthy

"The darker the night, the more evident the few stars twinkling between the clouds. The more awful be the state of professing Christendom as a whole, the more suitable is the background for the children of God to display their colors. The fiercer be the opposition made against a spiritual faith, the grander the opportunity for bringing forth its choicest fruit."[414]

~ A. W. Pink

"And others had trial of cruel mockings and scourgings, yea, moreover of bonds and imprisonment: They were stoned, they were sawn asunder, were tempted, were slain with the sword: they wandered about in sheepskins and goatskins; being destitute, afflicted, tormented" (Hebrews 11:36–37). Of these persecuted saints, the Hebrews author says, "Of whom the world was not worthy" (Hebrews 11:38).

> "Of whom the world was not worthy" is God's description of the very men whom the world casts out as fools or madmen.
> Dean Vaughan

The world (not the created universe, but that part of the world that is anti-God and organized to thwart His rule) counted and treated the great men and women of the faith (Hall of Faith in Hebrews 11) as unworthy (contemptible, as scum of the earth) and sought to silence or banish them through various ways. Albert Barnes says, "The world was so wicked that it had no claim that such holy men should live in it. It is at once a statement of their eminent holiness and of the wickedness of the rest of mankind."[415] With bitter and disgusting disdain the world yet views and treats believers. They are counted as troublers and irritators to the world's agenda, fanatical and foolish, unworthy of toleration.

Persecuted saints, despite the judgement of the world, outweigh it in value.[416] "'Of whom the world was not worthy" is God's description of the very men whom the world casts out as fools or madmen."[417] It is terminology used to turn the tables on worldly opinion and treatment of the Christian that says, "This man is not worthy of me or my attention; his values, ethics, beliefs, morality, and lifestyle fail to mesh with mine and are therefore to be ignored, mocked, insulted, marginalized, shunned, defamed, and demeaned."

However, it's the world that is unworthy of the Christian's presence, example, and benefits, not the opposite. "For they know not what a saint is, nor the worth of a saint, nor how to use him; they hate and drive such away, as they do the offer of Christ and his grace."[418] It's the judgement of God, not that of man, that matters; and He highly esteems (counts of great value, worth) the saint (Daniel 10:19; Proverbs 3:4; 1 Chronicles 29:17), saying that the world is not worthy of their association. Regardless of the status of the ungodly, they are inferior to the Christian, for it's not intellectual knowledge or worldly achievement that merits divine commendation and honor, but unwavering faith, allegiance, and holiness manifested to the triune God (Father, Son, and Holy Spirit) and the Holy Scriptures.

The ungodly, in discounting the saint as scum to be avoided and persecuted, brings harm to themselves. In fact, the persecuted may say to the persecutor, 'Weep not for us, but weep for yourselves' (Luke 23:28). Potiphar robbed himself of blessing and benefit in placing Joseph in prison (Genesis 39:20). Jezebel's cruel dictatorship and treatment of Elijah led to her excruciating death (2 Kings 9:33–35). The Jews, in rejection and persecution of Christ, forfeited salvation and great profit that He came to provide (John 1:11). The persecution and martyrdom of the saints deprive the world of comfort, peace of conscience, the message of hope, forgiveness and reconciliation to God through Christ, salt and light, and the means by which eternal torment may be avoided. Upon every instance that the ungodly extinguishes the "light" of a saint or tramples the "salt" of a saint beneath their feet, their circumstance and condition worsens. It is the saint's very presence in the world that restrains the hand of God in exacting severest judgment upon it and keeps it from being any worse than it is. Christians, as salt, serve as a preservative of the world by slowing down its moral and spiritual decay (Matthew 5:13). Remove it (Christians), and evil will have no restraint.

Although the world counts believers unworthy of existence, believers yet count the world worthy of their kindness, love, ministry, and even death (like Jesus Christ). And it is for His name's sake and the world's salvation (deliverance from spiritual darkness unto Him who is the Light) that saints endure cruel hatred and persecution.

30
Tortured for Christ

"To suffer persecution is to make things easier for those who are to follow. Today we enjoy the blessing of liberty because men in the past were willing to buy it for us at the cost of blood and sweat and tears. They made it easier for us, and by a steadfast and immovable witness for Christ, we may make it easier for others who are still to come."[419]

~ William Barclay

Sundar Singh. Singh was known as the "apostle with the bleeding feet" due to the lengthy distances he walked in sharing the Gospel throughout India. Persecution began at his conversion and continued throughout his life. His family renounced him, counting him as "dead." His sister poisoned him (miraculously he survived). He was arrested numerous times, bound in stocks, thrown into a dry well filled with decaying corpses and left to die, tied to a tree in a forest to die, and stoned. In 1929 Singh disappeared while making another missionary journey into the forbidden land of Tibet (he made 20 such trips). Sundar Singh said, "From my many years' experience, I can unhesitatingly say that the cross bears those who bear the cross."[420]

Dietrich Bonhoeffer. Bonhoeffer, a stout German Christian and biblical theologian, was active in rescuing Jews under the rule of Hitler in Germany and in conspiring to have him assassinated. In 1943 this resistance effort was discovered, and he was arrested. Bonhoeffer spent two years in the Tegel prison ministering to fellow inmates, corresponding to family and friends, and in the writing of *Letters and Papers from Prison*, a compilation of theological notes and correspondence that would be published several years after his death. He was transferred to the Buchenwald prison, then to the extermination camp at Flossenbürg, where he was executed by hanging on April 9, 1945.

A camp doctor that witnessed Bonhoeffer's hanging wrote: "The prisoners…were taken from their cells and the verdicts of court martial read out to them. Through the half-open door in one room of the huts, I saw Pastor Bonhoeffer, before taking off his prison garb, kneeling on the floor praying fervently to his God. I was most deeply moved by the way this lovable man prayed, so devout and so certain that God heard his prayer. At the place of execution, he again said a prayer and then climbed the steps to the gallows, brave and composed. His death ensued in a few seconds. In the almost 50 years that I have worked as a doctor, I have hardly ever seen a man die so entirely submissive to the will of God." Bonhoeffer's book *The Cost of Discipleship,* written in 1937, remains a Christian devotional classic.

Jim Elliot. Elliot was an American Christian missionary stationed in Shandia (Shan-dee-ah), a small Quichua (Kee-chew-wah) Indian village in Ecuador. Within three years many of the Quichuas had become devoted followers of Christ. It was at that point that Elliot decided it was time to give the message of Jesus to the Aucas, a tribal people that had killed many Quichuas and several workers at an oil-drilling site. Months of preparation and prayer ensued. Gifts regularly were lowered by bucket from an airplane to the Aucas, and friendly greetings in their language were voiced over an amplifier system. Surprisingly, the Aucas at one point sent a gift back up to the plane, something that prompted Elliot and the other four missionaries to seek a face-to-face encounter with them.

The first meeting happened four days after arriving. Three Aucas enjoyed a meal with them. On day six, January 8, 1956, a group of Auca warriors approached with spears to throw in hand. Although Elliot had a gun in his pocket, he refused to use it to save his life. (Each of them had made a promise not to kill an unsaved Auca to save his own life.) Within seconds the five missionaries, Ed McCully (age 28), Roger Youderian (age 31), Nate Saint (age 32), Pete Fleming (age 27) and Jim Elliot (age 28) were dead.[421] Elliot's words as a Wheaton College senior (1949) have impacted generations of missionaries and ministers: "He is no fool who gives what he cannot keep to gain what he cannot lose."[422] What is unknown to many is that their widows led their husband's killers to faith in Jesus Christ.[423]

Polycarp. Polycarp, the aged bishop of Smyrna, is among the most famous of martyrs. He was dragged by the mob to the tribunal of the Roman magistrate. Opportunity was given him to deny Christ and live or confess Christ and die. The proconsul urged him, saying, "Swear and I will release thee—reproach Christ." Polycarp answered, "Eighty and six years have I served Him, and He never once wronged me; how then shall I blaspheme my King, who hath saved me?" The proconsul again urged him, "Swear by the fortune of Caesar or be cast into the fire." Then said Polycarp, "You threaten me with fire, which burns for an hour and is soon extinguished, but the fire of the future judgment and of eternal punishment reserved for the ungodly you are ignorant of. But why do you delay? Do whatever you please." It was at that moment they took him to the stake and he prayed his last prayer: "O Lord God Almighty, the Father of Thy well-beloved and ever-blessed Son, by whom we have received the knowledge of Thee…I thank Thee that thou hast graciously thought me worthy of this day and of this hour." Polycarp's last words were: "O Father, I bless Thee that Thou hast counted me worthy to receive my portion among the martyrs."

Lambert. Lambert was a martyr under Henry VIII. While being consumed by a slow fire, he exclaimed, "None but Christ; none but Christ!"[424]

William Booth and the Salvation Army. Persecution and opposition to the salvationists were mild at the start (pelting with eggs as they preached) but intensified as the ministry expanded. (Such is always the case, let Christianity get a foothold in a society and all of Hell's fury will unite to stop it.) The *Skelton Army* attacked Booth and his soldiers violently in an effort to halt their preaching. Perhaps the worst of the attacks took place in Sheffield when a procession led by General Booth was assaulted by men with sticks and stones. At their hand Salvationists received bruised and bleeding faces.[425] "In twelve months, it is recorded, 669 Salvation-ists, of whom 251 were women, were 'knocked down, kicked, or brutally assaulted.' Fifty-six buildings of The Army were stormed and partially wrecked. Eighty-six Salvationists, fifteen of them women, were thrown into prison. From one end of the kingdom to the other, this effort to break up The Army was carried on in a most shameless fashion under the very eyes of the law: the mob attacking the Salvationists, the police arresting the Salvationists, the magistrates sentencing the Salvationists."[426] But the Salvationists were unstoppable and yet remain a force for righteousness.

Wrunken. In the 1500s, King Philip II of Spain signed a decree prohibiting the reading of the Bible in one's own language. Reports of violation surfaced in Flanders (present day Belgium). An officer was sent to investigate and, if necessary, exact judgement. It was discovered that Wrunken, a 13-year-old girl, owned a Bible. Knowing that such possession meant death, she nevertheless said, "This book is mine. I am reading from it, and it is more precious to me than anything!" Swiftly she was imprisoned and then sentenced to die by suffocation. A place in the city wall was hollowed out whereto she would be tied. To the offer provided to save herself by repenting, she replied, "My Savior died for me. I will also die for Him." Inside the hollowed wall, as bricks were laid higher and higher, another offer of release was presented. Again, the young girl rejected it, saying, "I will be with Jesus." Finally, the wall was finished except for one last brick that would cover her face. The pleading official for a final time said, "Repent. Just say the word and you will go free." Wrunken refused, saying, "O Lord, forgive my murderers." The brick was put in place, and she suffocated as a martyr for our Lord.[427]

Lawrence Saunders. Martyred by the "bloody Queen Mary," Saunders' final words were "Welcome the cross of Christ! Welcome the cross of Christ! Welcome life everlasting!"[428]

Hugh Latimer. As Hugh Latimer and Nicholas Ridley were both about to be burned as heretics for their teachings and beliefs outside Balliol College, Oxford (16 October, 1555), Latimer exclaimed, "Be of good comfort, Master Ridley, and *play the man!* We shall this day light such a candle, by God's grace, in England, as I trust shall never be put out."[429]

William Tyndale. Tyndale provided the first English Bible based upon the original Hebrew and Greek texts. Following a year of imprisonment in 1535 for heresy, Tyndale was executed by strangulation and his body burned at the stake (1536). His final prayer was in behalf of the King of England, that his eyes would be opened to the truth of the Holy Scriptures. Within a year after his death, the prayer was answered, as King Henry authorized the "Matthew Bible," a work that was largely Tyndale's.[430]

John Wesley. Throughout most of Wesley's ministry he was pelted with rotten tomatoes, manure, and stones, and his soft hair yanked. He often was pursued by men with deadly and injurious instruments in hand. In 1738, the church banned Wesley's preaching, forcing it into the open fields and other venues. Not only was he disbarred from the church but mocked and criticized by the faculty and students at his alma mater for his sermon *Scriptural Christianity* (1744). It's painful to be maligned, harangued and harassed by "outsiders" but even more so to experience it at the hands of fellow believers. Yet despite the persecution that arose from "within and without," Wesley refused to quit, lighting a torch for Christ that burns brightly today not only through "Methodism" but all of the evangelical world.

John Huss. Huss was arrested, condemned, and sentenced to be burned at the stake in 1415. Upon hearing the sentence, he went to his knees and prayed, "Lord Jesus, forgive my enemies." Chained to the stake, he prayed, "In Thee, O Lord, do I put my trust; let me never be ashamed."[431]

John Bradford. On July 1, 1555, John Bradford, one the most popular preachers of that time, was burned at the stake for his faith. For the entire distance from West London to Newgate, the place of his execution, Bradford shouted: "Christ; Christ; none but Christ!"[432]

Cyprian. Having been banished, Cyprian suffered martyrdom in Carthage in 258. Upon hearing the news of the sentence of his death, he said, "I heartily thank Almighty God who is pleased to set me free from the chains of the body."[433]

Obadiah Holmes. Holmes (1607–1682) was evicted from Massachusetts because of his Baptist beliefs, settling in Newport, Rhode Island. In 1651, Holmes and two friends, upon having communion with a blind man in Massachusetts, were arrested for unlawful worship. They were sentenced to either a whipping or a fine. Clarke and Crandall paid their fines, but Holmes refused. On September 6, 1651, Obadiah Holmes was severely beaten with thirty stripes. As the whip came down upon his back, Holmes declared, "I am now come to be baptized in afflictions by your hands, that so I may have further fellowship with my Lord. I am not ashamed of His sufferings, for by His stripes am I healed." One commentator says he was whipped "unmercifully." Yet following his beating, Holmes turned to the magistrates and said, "You have struck me with roses." Governor Jenks observed that "for many days, if not some weeks, he could take no rest but upon his knees and elbows, not being able to suffer any part of his body to touch the bed whereupon he lay." Speaking of his punishment later, Holmes testified, "As the strokes fell upon me, I had such a spiritual manifestation of God's presence as the like thereof I never had nor felt, nor can fleshly tongue express; and the outward pain was so removed from me that indeed I am not able to declare it, yea, and in a manner felt it not, although it was grievous, as the spectators said, the man striking with all his strength (yea, spitting in his hand three times, as many affirmed) with a three-corded whip, giving me therewith thirty strokes."[434]

John Bunyan. Bunyan, suffering persecution in a Bedford prison, wrote, "Therefore, I bind these lies and slanderous accusations to my person as an ornament. It belongs to my Christian profession to be vilified, slandered, reproached and reviled; and since all this isnothing but that, as God and my conscience testify, I rejoice in being reproached for Christ's sake."

Clement Shahbaz Bhatti. "I made it clear that I will consider— this is the important phrase I am trying to say—myself most fortunate if Jesus Christ will accept the sacrifice of my blood to raise the voice for the justice and rights of the persecuted and victimized

Christians and other minorities in Pakistan."[435] She was martyred in Islamabad in 2011 as a "blasphemer" of Muhammad.

Martin Luther. Luther, despite threats of punishment if he did not recant his belief, said, "My conscience is the prisoner to the Word of God. I cannot and will not recant. Here I stand; I can do none other. God help me." The stand resulted in his excommunication from the church by the pope and condemnation as an outlaw by the emperor.

Similar tortures of believers are being exacted presently throughout the world.

31
Persecution Prospers Christendom

"It is strange that you can always trace the progress of the church by a trail of blood."[436]

~ Alan Redpath

Jesus said, "I tell you the truth, unless a kernel of wheat is planted in the soil and dies, it remains alone. But its death will produce many new kernels—a plentiful harvest of new lives" (John 12:24 NLT). The martyrdom of Stephen by stoning advanced the church. Saith John MacArthur, "He is great proof that the effect of a man's life or ministry has nothing to do with the length of it. His ministry was so short, and yet it was the catalyst that caused the church to move out in the next step in its commission and reach Judea and Samaria with the Gospel. Stephen was the trigger that shot the church into the world. And I don't think that anybody can fully estimate the results of even a brief work of one man, when that one man has the courage to do and say what he knows is right whatever the consequences."[437]

Spurgeon states, "Never did the church so much prosper and so truly thrive as when she was baptized in the blood. The ship of the church never sails so gloriously along as when the bloody spray of her martyrs falls on her deck. We must suffer and we must die, if we are ever to conquer this world for Christ."[438] John Piper comments, "God makes persecution serve the unstoppable mission of the church—your mission, your ministry."[439] He uses the persecution and suffering of His people to spread the Gospel throughout the world (2 Corinthians 4:7–12). The truth of God cannot be eradicated through the persecution of His followers. It only inflames and prospers it, a fact revealed in history. Truth though suppressed through persecution, ultimately prevails. At the first, the killings of Ed McCully, Roger Youderian, Nate Saint, Pete Fleming, and Jim Elliot on January 8, 1956, by Auca warriors in Ecuador seemed needless. However, years later the seed they planted with their "blood" out of love for the Aucas sprang forth into the glorious harvest of bringing Aucas into the kingdom of God.

Tertullian said, "The oftener we are mown down by you, the more in number we grow. The blood of Christians is seed."[440] Saith Tertullian also, "The bloods of the martyrs are the seeds of the church. Continued in the torture, they increased in number more than those who were killed. 'Verily, verily, I say unto you, except a corn of wheat fall into the ground and die, it abideth alone: but if it die, it bringeth forth much fruit' (John 12:24). The more severe the punishment, the more people were added to the Christian faith. Our Lord Jesus Christ sent out His apostles as sheep among wolves. Did the Lord not care that those wolves will kill His sheep? No. What happened was the opposite. In devouring the sheep, the wolves became sheep."[441] Harry Ironside says, "The testimony of the dying again and again led their very persecutors to receive the Lord Jesus Christ as their Savior because of the convincing power of the truth manifested in the martyrs. Satan's effort to destroy Christianity by persecution was in vain."[442]

Hitler's persecution of the Jews illustrates the truth. German pastor Hermann Gruner said, "The time is fulfilled for the German people of Hitler. It is because of Hitler that Christ, God the helper and redeemer, has become effective among us....Hitler is the way of the Spirit and the will of God for the German people to enter the Church of Christ." Another pastor stated: "Christ has come to us through Adolph Hitler."[443] Jim Denison told a Cuban pastor of his sorrow over the persecution Cuban Christians were suffering and that he was praying for it to lessen. Surprisingly, the pastor requested that such intercession cease, explaining that persecution was strengthening his people and purifying their faith.[444]

Albert Barnes wrote, "It has become a settled principle that nothing which is good and true can be destroyed by persecution, but that the effect ultimately is to establish more firmly and to spread more widely that which it was designed to overthrow. It has long since passed into a proverb that 'the blood of the martyrs is the seed of the church.'"[445] W. A. Criswell, speaking of Stephen's martyr-dom, said, "Stephen's life and influence endured as a Christian's life and influence always endures. It never fails; it never fades; it never falls into uselessness or vanity or futility or frustration. God sees to that. As Hebrews 11:4 says, "He being dead yet speaketh."

No word for Christ ever falls to the ground; it has its repercussion in the purposes of God. And no life ever laid down for Christ was ever laid down in vain. God blesses it. Look at this man Stephen. It seems it would look as if his life was lost, stoned to death. But look what God did with it. Those who were crying the defamation and condemnation of Stephen laid down their clothes [outer garments] at the feet of a young man named Saul [Acts 7:58]."[446] Witnessing and consenting to Stephen's martyrdom, something was buried in Paul's heart that he never was able to shake and that ultimately played a role in his conversion (Acts 22:20). Through Stephen's death, life sprung forth in a man that impacted the world for Christ as none other. Saul the persecutor became Paul the preacher.

Farrar states, "And mark that when the bad, hating the good, sneer them out of court, repress them by violence, madden the blind multitude by lies against them, poison them as Socrates was poisoned, banish them as Epictetus was banished, burn them as Savonarola was burned, execrate them as Whitfield was execrated, do not think that then the good have failed. Even in their ashes live their wonted fires; their voices even from the grave sound in the thunder's mouth. Their dead hands pull down the stronghold of their enemies, and tyrants tremble at their ghosts."[447] John Foxe said, "Princes, kings, and other rulers of the world have used all their strength and cunning against the Church, yet it continues to endure and hold its own."[448]

Praise be unto God that His Truth is unstoppable, though His followers be pelleted with stones, burned at the stake, crucified, ridiculed, imprisoned, or have body members severed. With historians, prophets, kings and the persecuted past and present we join them in saying,

Mine eyes have seen the glory of the coming of the Lord;
He is trampling out the vintage where the grapes of wrath are stored;
He hath loosed the fateful lightning of His terrible swift sword;
His truth is marching on.

Glory, glory, hallelujah!
Glory, glory, hallelujah!
Glory, glory, hallelujah!
His truth is marching on.

I have seen Him in the watchfires of a hundred circling camps;
They have builded Him an altar in the evening dews and damps;
I can read His righteous sentence by the dim and flaring lamps;
His day is marching on.

He has sounded forth the trumpet that shall never call retreat;
He is sifting out the hearts of all before His judgment seat.
Oh, be swift, my soul, to answer Him; be jubilant, my feet!
Our God is marching on.

In the beauty of the lilies Christ was born across the sea
With a glory in His bosom that transfigures you and me.
As He died to make us holy, let us die to make all free,
While God is marching on.

~ Julia Ward Howe (1862)

32
Victors and Heroes

"My prison has become a palace!"[449]
~ *Perpetua* (Christian martyr of the 3rd century)

The persecuted saints, despite cruel and barbaric suffering for Christ or death, are victors and heroes. Christians are "more than conquerors" through Jesus Christ (Romans 8:37). Even though crucified, stoned, stabbed, dragged, skinned and burned, their voice is not silenced; nor is their cause impeded. In fact, history teaches the church thrives under such hostile and barbaric treatment.

A biblical pattern for conquest in persecution is well illustrated and displayed by Shadrach, Meshach, and Abed-nego upon their refusal to bow to the image of gold erected by King Nebuchadnezzar (Daniel 3).

They were confident. "Our God whom we serve is able to deliver us from the burning fiery furnace" (Daniel 3:17). The persecuted saint says with David, "For you have been my hope, Sovereign LORD, my confidence since my youth" (Psalm 71:5 NIV), and with Isaiah, "Behold, God is my salvation; I will trust, and not be afraid: for the Lord Jehovah is my strength and my song; he also is become my salvation" (Isaiah 12:2). Knowing that God is with us in the unjust treatment makes it bearable, endurable. William Tyndale said, "For if God be on our side, what matter maketh it who be against us, be they bishops, cardinals, popes, or whatsoever names they will?"[450]

"Imagine you are on a high cliff," writes Tim Keller, "and you lose your footing and begin to fall. Just beside you is a branch sticking out of the edge of the cliff. It is your only hope and seems more than strong enough. How can it save you? If you're certain the branch can support you, but you don't actually reach out and grab it, you are lost. If instead your mind is filled with doubts and uncertainty that the branch can hold you, but you reach out and grab it anyway, you will be saved. Why? It is not the strength of your faith but the object of your faith that actually saves you. Strong faith in a weak branch is fatally inferior to weak faith in a strong branch."[451] Obviously, the idea is to have strong faith in a strong branch, but even little faith in a strong branch avails much. Recall the words of Jesus, "Verily I say unto you, If ye have faith as a grain of mustard seed, ye shall say unto this mountain, Remove hence to yonder place; and it shall remove; and nothing shall be impossible unto you" (Matthew 17:20).

Matthew Henry says that the text, "refers to the quantity: 'If you had but a grain of true faith, though so little that it were like that which is the least of all seeds, you would do wonders.' Faith in general is a firm assent to, a compliance with, and a confidence in, all divine revelation."[452] Albert Barnes comments, "The mustard seed was the smallest of all seeds. There is a principle of vitality in the grain of seed stretching forward to great results, which illustrates the nature of faith. Your faith should be like that."[453]

The writer of Hebrews says that it was through faith in God's promises that the early saints endured the severity of persecution and even death. Saith Hebrews 11:33–39, "Who through faith (he does not indicate its measure) subdued kingdoms, wrought righteousness, obtained promises, stopped the mouths of lions, Quenched the violence of fire, escaped the edge of the sword, out of weakness were made strong, waxed valiant in fight, turned to flight the armies of the aliens. Women received their dead raised to life again: and others were tortured, not accepting deliverance; that they might obtain a better resurrection: And others had trial of cruel mockings and scourgings, yea, moreover of bonds and imprisonment: They were stoned, they were sawn asunder, were tempted, were slain with the sword: they wandered about in sheepskins and goatskins; being destitute, afflicted, tormented; (Of whom the world was not worthy:) they wandered in deserts, and in mountains, and in dens and caves of the earth. And these all, having obtained a good report through faith." As with these martyrs, "By faith we are made strong at the root like the seaweed that grows on the rock, no matter how much it may be lashed hither and thither by the ceaseless action of the waves."[454]

They were concrete. "O king, that we will not serve thy gods, nor worship the golden image which thou hast set up" (Daniel 3:18). They were firm in their decision not to compromise belief or dishonor God. Their minds could not be changed regardless of pressure or pain. Manifest a fixed and steadfast mind not to "bend or bow" to pressure and threats to deny the Lord. Don't waver or wobble.

They were clever. Upon being asked by Nebuchadnezzar to give reason for their decision not to bow to the image, the Hebrew children wisely replied, "We are not careful to answer thee in this matter" (Daniel 3:16). The word "careful" means "of necessity"; it was unnecessary for them to cite the reasons for refusal to worship the idol or vindicate themselves.[455] Their decision was unalterable and unchangeable. Nothing said either by the king or themselves would change their mind. To deliberate with a persecutor (when his mind is decided) spawns the chance of caving to compromise. Be smart enough to realize that such is futile and opens the door to temptation.

They were compliant. It was their duty, as with every Christian, to stand for God, regardless of its cost and consequence (Daniel 3:17). And this they did.

> Living for Jesus wherever I am,
> Doing each duty in His holy name,
> Willing to suffer affliction and loss,
> Deeming each trial a part of my cross.
> ~ Thomas Obediah Chisholm (1917)

They were courageous. Feeling the heat and seeing the burning furnace to which they were to be cast, Shadrach, Meshach and Abed-nego said boldly, "Be it known unto thee, O king, that we will not serve thy gods, nor worship the golden image which thou hast set up" (Daniel 3:18).

They were congenial. "Be it known unto thee, O king" (Daniel 3:18). In response to the harshness, rage and anger exacted by the king (Daniel 3:13–15), they manifested respect and kindness. The persecuted saint must heed the instruction of Jesus in making response to persecutors: "But I say unto you, love your enemies, bless them that curse you, do good to them that hate you, and pray for them which despitefully use you, and persecute you" (Matthew 5:44). Don't dish out what they give out. Do the opposite.

They were calm. "Shadrach, Meshach, and Abednego replied, 'O Nebuchadnezzar, we are not worried about what will happen to us'" (Daniel 3:16 TLB). Trust in God banishes fear. The persecuted saint says with Jeremiah, "But the Lord is with me like a mighty warrior; so my persecutors will stumble and not prevail. They will fail and be thoroughly disgraced; their dishonor will never be forgotten" (Jeremiah 20:11 NIV). Saith Spurgeon, "To throw the Christian into the furnace is to put him into Christ's parlor; for lo! Jesus Christ is walking with him."[456]

When saints of God in danger stood,
    He to their rescue came;
He joined them in the furnace hot
    And quenched the raging flame.

He saw their courage and faith;
    He read their noble aim;
He quickly came to meet their need
    And quenched the raging flame.

The fires are kindled all around;
    Our foes are still the same,
But God will come, if we are true,
    And quench the raging flame.

When thro' the fire thy path shall lie,
    Press on in Jesus' name;
For He has promised to be near
    And quench the raging flame.

~ H. J. Zelley (1901)

In acknowledging that God orders the steps of the righteous, that nothing ultimately happens to the righteous without His permission, that it is the Lord that fights our battles (as our "Mighty Warrior") and that all things work together for the good; calm and peace are automatics. "That grace," comments Matthew Henry, "which was sufficient for them [the prophets and saints before us], to carry them through their sufferings, shall not be deficient to you."[457]

33
The Climax to Persecution

"Soon the battle will be over. It will not be long now before the day will come when Satan will no longer trouble us. There will be no more domination, temptation, accusation, or confrontation [persecution]. Our warfare will be over and our commander, Jesus Christ, will call us away from the battlefield to receive the victor's crown."[458]
~ Thomas Watson

An end will come to the horrendous suffering and mistreatment of persecuted believers. An ending to persecution comes by promotion to Heaven (death). Paul's final persecution was imprisonment in Rome where he expected execution—"my departure is at hand" (2 Timothy 4:6). Though the manner of Paul's death is an unknown, it's plausible to believe that he was beheaded at the order of the Roman emperor Nero. Eusebius (A.D. 265–339), historian of Christianity, embraced that view. In departing the world, Paul said, "I have fought the good fight, I have finished the race, I have kept the faith. Finally, there is laid up for me the crown of righteousness, which the Lord, the righteous Judge, will give to me on that Day, and not to me only but also to all who have loved His appearing" (2 Timothy 4:7–8 NKJV). Good news! Persecution may last for the night, but eternal deliverance and reward come in the morning. "Therefore endure hardness, as a good soldier of Jesus Christ" (2 Timothy 2:3). With Paul, regardless of oppression or martyrdom, "keep the faith" until the end. The final adversity is not far away that will usher you into Christ's presence victoriously where the "Crown of Life" will be presented and Heaven's joy forever experienced. When D. L. Moody lay dying, he looked up to Heaven and said, "Earth is receding; Heaven is opening. This is my coronation day."

My race is run; my warfare's o'er;
    The solemn hour is nigh,
When, offered up to God, my soul
    Shall wing its flight on high.

With heav'nly weapons I have fought
  The battles of the Lord,
Finished my course and kept the faith,
  Depending on His Word.

Henceforth there is laid up for me
  A crown which cannot fade;
The righteous Judge at that great day
  Shall place it on my head.

Nor hath the Sov'reign Lord decreed
  This prize for me alone,
But for all such as love like me
  Th' appearance of His Son.

From ev'ry snare and evil work
  His grace shall me defend,
And to His heav'nly kingdom safe
  Shall bring me in the end.

~ Isaac Watts

The Scottish Presbyterian Covenanters (Christians that revolted against the monarch's claim of authority over the church in Scotland), in dying for their faith, would often climb the scaffold shouting, "Good-bye world! Good-bye pain! Good-bye suffering! Good-bye sorrow! Good-bye heartache! Welcome life! Welcome joy! Welcome Heaven! Welcome eternity! Welcome Jesus!"[459] All the persecuted saints of God can "shout" the same as they make their heavenly exodus.

An ending to persecution comes by the return of Christ. In Paul's closing exhortation to the Romans he says, "The God of peace will soon crush Satan under your feet" (Romans 16:20 NIV). Compare with Genesis 3:15. Multitudes of persecuted saints will be delivered from persecution at the return of Christ (Satan's absolute and total defeat) that is imminent (likely to happen at any moment). "The Lord is coming soon" (Philippians 4:5 NCV). At His return, Satan, with all his evil host, will be utterly crushed and defeated (Revelation 20:10).

Spurgeon states, "To be despised and rejected of men is the Christian's lot. I tell you if you look for your reward to Christ's bride herself you will miss it; if you expect to receive your crown from the hand even of your brethren in the ministry who know your labors and who ought to sympathize with your trials, you will be mistaken. 'When the King shall come in his glory,' then is your time of recompense; but not today, nor tomorrow, nor at any time in this world. Reckon nothing which you acquire, no honor which you gain, to be the reward of your service to your Master; that is reserved to the time 'when the King shall come in his glory.'"[460]

Saith W. A. Criswell, "'Lord, when will You cast out evil? When will death be no more? When will the usurper, Satan, be destroyed? When will the righteous be vindicated? Lord, when will our new kingdom be given to Thy saints? Lord, when? How long? How long?' (Revelation 6:10). And the Lord replies, 'In a little while' (Revelation 6:11), in a little while, just a little while. And while we are waiting, of course, it seems long. But it isn't. But it isn't. Just a little while, just a little while. 'And He that shall come will come, and will not tarry' (Hebrews 10:37). In just a little while, God shall vindicate His people. In just a little while, sin and death will be cast out (Revelation 20:14). In just a little while, we shall see our Savior; we shall be resurrected and glorified (1 Thessalonians 4:16–17). We shall find our place in His presence. We shall live with God's people in glory, "in a little while," in a little while (John 16:16). And that is their prayer—as it is ours. 'O Lord, that Thy kingdom might come' and that God's will might be done in this sin-cursed earth as it is done in God's beautiful Heaven (Matthew 6:9–10)."[461] Amen and amen.

> Blessed are they that for His sake
>   Are persecuted and reviled;
> Our Savior's love a Heav'n can make,
>   When storms of earth are fierce and wild.

~ Persecuted for Christ's Sake ~

Oh, thoughts of Him who bore the cross
   Should teach our hearts to bear with joy
Their burdens, tho' in pain and loss,
    Whatever ills of earth annoy!
    Whatever ills of earth annoy!
Blessed are they! Blessed are they!

Blessed are they that for His sake
   Are persecuted and reviled;
May nothing here our courage shake,
   While on we bear His yoke so mild.

Oh, still be faithful to the last,
   Untempted e'en amid despair!
Tho' round the faithful snares are cast,
   Theirs is Heav'n's kingdom, bright and fair.
   Theirs is Heav'n's kingdom, bright and fair.
Blessed are they! Blessed are they!

                ~ George Cooper (1873)

34
Lessons from the Persecuted Church at Smyrna

"Here am I; send me. Send me to the ends of the earth; send me to the rough, the savage lost of the wilderness; send me from all that is called comfort on earth; send me even to death itself, if it be but in Your service and to promote Your kingdom."[462]
~ David Brainerd

A fitting summary and conclusion to this book is found in the words of the angel to the saints at Smyrna. The angel said, "Do not be afraid of what you are about to suffer" (Revelation 2:10a NIV). The church was suffering persecution, literally a pressure unto death, for failure to worship Caesar and other pagan gods, something that would only intensify (Revelation 2:10b). Regarding the persecution, note what saith the Holy Scriptures.

They were not to be exempt from it ("what you are about to suffer"). Adrian Rogers said, "The church will know more and more persecution. There is no way you can be a genuine Christian and be exempt."[463] "Yea, and all that will live godly in Christ Jesus shall suffer persecution" (2 Timothy 3:12).

They were not to be afraid of it ("do not be afraid"). Lottie Moon said, "Only believe; don't fear. Our Master, Jesus, always watches over us, and no matter what the persecution, Jesus will surely overcome it."[464]

They were to be encouraged by the brevity of it ("you will suffer persecution for ten days"). Persecution is an experience that lasts briefly ("ten days") in contrast to eternity. Albert Barnes says, "A short time; a brief period; a few days. It is possible, indeed, that this might have been literally ten days, but it is much more in accordance with the general character of this book, in regard to numbers, to suppose that the word 'ten' here is used to denote a few."[465] Criswell says it refers to intensity of persecution rather than its duration.[466]

My take is that it was to be intense, severe suffering that in contrast to eternity will be short in duration. Paul echoes the same in saying, "Our light affliction, which is but for a moment" (2 Corinthians 4:17). The saint's suffering, in contrast to Heaven's eternal glory, is short. Albert Barnes says, "Affliction in this life, however severe, can be but brief; and in the hope that it will soon end, why should we not bear it without complaining or repining?"[467]

They would be comforted in it. W. A. Criswell says, "He comforts them by the words of introduction He says about Himself: 'I am the First and the Last' (Revelation 2:8). Before the days of trial began, and throughout the days of this furious, furious burning and beyond, 'I am the First and the Last,' through it all, through it all, their living Lord and ours; 'I am the First and the Last,' with you all the way through."[468]

Second, He comforts them in saying, "I know thy tribulation" (Revelation 2:9 ASV). I know what you are up against. I know the crushing pressure of pain and hardship that is borne. To know that He knows our suffering and promises to sustain us through it grants great hope and consolation. And in the third place, the saint is comforted in persecution in knowing that every hostile action experienced is an offering of love and devotion to Christ. H. A. Ironside states, "Smyrna means 'myrrh.' It is frequently mentioned in Scripture in connection with the embalming of the dead. Myrrh had to be crushed in order to give out its fragrance. When God's people were being crushed like myrrh, what a sweet odor of devotion, what fragrance of Christian love was wafted up to the very throne of God!"[469]

They were not to dread it. "We need not dread suffering," Albert Barnes states, "if we can hear the voice of the Redeemer encouraging us, and if He assures us that in a little while we shall have the crown of life."[470]

They were to be faithful through it—"Be faithful unto death" (Revelation 2:10 ESV)—not fits and starts, but steadfastness in confession of Christ. Adam Clarke says, "Be firm, hold fast the faith, confess Christ to the last and at all hazards."[471] Caleb Morris states, "Fidelity must not give way at any future point of life. No event can justify its suspension for a moment. It must stand even the fiery test of martyrdom."[472] Prepare to be ready to stand firm and immoveable in the faith. "Say 'Yes' before your fears have time to shape 'No.' Say 'No' before your inclinations have time to whisper 'Yes.'"[473]

A Christian prisoner in Cuba was asked to sign a statement containing accusations against brethren which would lead to their arrest. He said, "The chain keeps me from signing this."

The communist officer protested, "But you are not in chains!"

"I am," said the Christian. "I am bound by the chain of witnesses who throughout the centuries gave their lives for Jesus Christ. I am a link in this chain. I will not break it."[474]

They would be rewarded for it—"I will give you the crown of life" (Revelation 2:10 ESV). An eternal and happy life with a special reward (commendation) awaits saints in Heaven at the conclusion of their temporal suffering. See Chapter 11, *The Crown of Life.*

They would be preserved from the "second death" because of it. "He that overcometh shall not be hurt of the second death" (Revelation 2:11). John asks, "Who is he that overcometh the world?" (I John 5:5a). And then he answers the question, saying, "He that believeth that Jesus is the Son of God" (1 John 5:5b). The Christian is the "overcomer." Though not exempt from the first death (physical), believers (the redeemed, born-again, regenerated by Christ) are preserved from the "second death" which removes the soul eternally from the presence of God and hope of Heaven to an abode in Hell. Persecution *confirms* salvation; it does not *secure* it.

I mean to go right on until the crown is won;
I mean to fight the fight of faith till life on earth is done.
I'll nevermore turn back; defeat I shall not know,
For God will give me victory, if onward I shall go.

I'm going on; I'm going on;
Unto the final triumph, I'm going on.
I'm going on; I'm going on;
Unto the final triumph, I'm going on.

~ Persecuted for Christ's Sake ~

Should opposition come, should foes obstruct my way,
Should persecution's fires be lit, as in the ancient day—
With Jesus by my side, His peace within my soul,
No matter if the battle's hot, I mean to win the goal.

I see a shining crown awaiting over there;
I see a mansion all prepared and decked with beauties rare.
Shall that which intervenes deprive me of my right?
Nay, on I'll go until I reach that city of delight.

Then forward let us go, our hearts with love aflame,
Our snowy banner borne aloft, inscribed with Jesus' name.
The hosts of evil flee, and Heaven's open gates
Invite me now to hasten where eternal glory waits.

~ Charles W. Naylor (1918)

"Yes! Onward, Christian! The captain of your salvation hath gone through the dark valley before you—therefore, onward! Onward with boldness! Onward with courage! Onward with hope! that ye may be like your Savior by participation in his sufferings."[475]

~ C. H. Spurgeon

"Do not be afraid, but go on speaking and do not be silent, for I am with you."

~ Acts 18:9-10 ESV

Endnotes

[1] https://www.rylequotes.org/quotes/laughter-ridicule-opposition-and-persecution, accessed February 27, 2021.

[2] Ferguson, Sinclair. *The Sermon on the Mount.* (Carlisle, PA: Banner of Truth, 1997), 41.

[3] MacArthur, John. "How to Handle Persecution, Part 1." gty.com, accessed April 11, 2021.

[4] Watson, Thomas. *The Beatitudes: Concerning Persecution.* https://www.gracegems.org/Watson/beatitudes9.htm, accessed April 6, 2021.

[5] Interview on the 700 Club, February 16, 2016. https://www.youtube.com/watch?v=qJGSc4ZSlIM, accessed April 19, 2021.

[6] The Character Journal. www.characterjournal.com, accessed April 16, 2021.

[7] https://decisionmagazine.com/global-picture-faith-suffering/, accessed May 21, 2021

[8] Exell, J. S. *The Biblical Illustrator:* Acts. (Grand Rapids, MI: Baker Book House, 1952), 5:41.

[9] Matthew 5:11.

[10] Byrley, Christopher. "Persecution and the 'Adversary' of 1 Peter 5:8." *The Southern Baptist Journal of Theology,* SBJT 21/3 (Fall 2017).

[11] Zodhiates, S. *The Complete Word Study Dictionary: New Testament* (electronic ed.). (Chattanooga, TN: AMG Publishers, 2000).

[12] Spence-Jones, H. D. M. (Ed.). *St. Matthew* (Vol. 1). (London; New York: Funk & Wagnalls Company, 1909), 150.

[13] Gardner, R. B. *Matthew.* (Scottdale, PA: Herald Press, 1991), 98.

[14] Swindoll, Chuck. "Our Common Struggles: Affliction, Confusion, Persecution," August 29, 2018. www. Insight.org, accessed February 15, 2021.

[15] Christian Persecution. https://www.opendoorsusa.org/christian-persecution/, accessed March 19, 2021.

[16] George Whitefield. "Persecution Every Christian's Lot," (sermon). https://www.blueletterbible.org/Comm/whitefield_george/Sermons/witf_055.cfm, accessed April 19, 2021.

[17] Carson, D. A. *The Expositor's Bible Commentary: Matthew, Mark, Luke* (Vol. 8). F. E. Gaebelein (Ed.). (Grand Rapids: Zondervan Publishing House, 1984), 137.

[18] Maclaren, Alexander. *Expositions of Scripture,* Vol. 16, (Hebrews 7 to 1 John 4). "Resisting unto Blood," 213.

[19] Spurgeon, C. H. *Morning and Evening,* November 10 (Evening).

[20] Graham, Billy. *Decision*, "Do You Bear the Marks of Christ?," (Charlotte, N. C.: The Billy Graham Evangelistic Association, 2006), December.

[21] Cochran, Gregory C. "Christian Persecution as Explained by Jesus" (Matthew 5:10-12). SBJT-18.1-Christian-Persecution-as-Explained-by-Jesus-Matthew-5-10-12.pdf, 11. Accessed March 10, 2021.

[22] Ibid.

[23] Simeon, C. *Horae Homileticae:* Matthew (Vol. 11). (London: Holdsworth and Ball, 1832–1863), 457–458.

[24] Ferguson, Everett, (Ed.). *Encyclopedia of Early Christianity:* Second Edition. (New York and London: Routledge Taylor and Francis Group, 1999), Under entry Martyr, Martyrdom.

[25] Christian Persecution. https://www.opendoorsusa.org/christian-persecution/, accessed March 19, 2021.

[26] See, for example, "Rising Restrictions on Religion," published by The Pew Research Center's Forum on Religion and Public Life, August 2011. This report documents 130 countries in which Christians are officially targeted for harassment or other forms of persecution. This was the highest number of countries for any religion (Gregory C. Cochran).

[27] "Persecuted for Christ!" https://savethepersecutedchristians.org/persecution-by-the-numbers/, accessed February 11, 2021.

[28] https://www.persecution.org/, accessed February 5, 2021.

[29] ChristianPost.com.

[30] *Dereset News.* "Christian Killed Every Five Minutes." September 2, 2011. www.deresetnews.com, accessed March 13, 2015.

[31] https://www.azquotes.com/quote/1404937, accessed May 7, 2021.

[32] Spurgeon, C. H. "The Sieve" (Sermon delivered January 1, 1874), Matthew 7:21. https://www.spurgeon.org/resource-library/sermons/the-sieve-2/#flipbook/, accessed March 2, 2021.

[33] MacArthur, John. "Twelve Ordinary Men" (sermon delivered October 11, 2009). https://www.gty.org/library/sermons-library/41-14/twelve-ordinary-men, accessed May 8, 2021.

[34] "Persecution." *Holman Bible Dictionary,* published by Broadman & Holman, 1991.

[35] "Persecution." *Naves Topical Index.*

[36] MacArthur, John. *The Book on Leadership,* (Nashville: Thomas Nelson, 2004), 130.

[37] https://factober.com/quotes/quote/persecution-is-one-of-the-natural-consequences-of-living-the-christian-life-f8f9db, accessed April 7, 2021.

[38] https://www.jcryle.info/2015/11/, accessed February 27, 2021.

[39] Plumer, W. S. *Studies in the Book of Psalms: Being a Critical and Expository Commentary, with Doctrinal and Practical Remarks on the Entire Psalter.* (Philadelphia; Edinburgh: J. B. Lippincott Company; A & C Black. 1872), 1041.

[40] Bonhoeffer, Dietrich. The Cost of Discipleship. (New York: MacMillan Publishing Company, 1963..

[41] Video. *We Stand With Them.* https://www.youtube.com/watch?v= nDqqnuW57zc, accessed February 11, 2021.

[42] Ann Lovell, posted May 26, 2020, in *International Mission Board,* "Prayer," SBC News, The Persecuted Church.

[43] Jeremiah, David. "The Increase of Intolerance." https://sermons.love/david-jeremiah/586-david-jeremiah-the-increase-of-intolerance.html, accessed February 10, 2021.

[44] Rogers, Adrian. "Preparing for the Coming Persecution" (Sermon). https://www.oneplace.com/ministries/love-worth-finding/read/articles/preparing-for-the-coming-persecution-17488.html, accessed February 5, 2021.

[45] Carson, D. A. *The Expositor's Bible Commentary: Matthew, Mark, Luke* (Vol. 8). F. E. Gaebelein (Ed.). (Grand Rapids: Zondervan Publishing House, 1984), 135.

[46] Byrley, Christopher. "Persecution and the 'Adversary' of 1 Peter 5:8." *The Southern Baptist Journal of Theology,* SBJT 21/3 (Fall 2017).

[47] Spurgeon, C. H. "The War of Truth" (January 11, 1857), *New Park Street Pulpit,* Volume 3.

[48] *Notes on the Bible* by Albert Barnes [1834], Ephesians 6:12.

[49] Byrley, Christopher. "Persecution and the 'Adversary' of 1 Peter 5:8." *The Southern Baptist Journal of Theology,* SBJT 21/3 (Fall 2017).

[50] Calvin, John. *John Calvin's Commentaries,* Matthew 5:10.

[51] *Preaching Magazine,* July 9, 2018, Illustrations. https://preaching.org/pm_illustrations/truth/, accessed May 7, 2021.

[52] Pink, A. W. *An Exposition of Hebrews.* (Swengel, PA: Bible Truth Depot, 1954), 860.

[53] Ibid.

[54] Ibid.

[55] Spurgeon, C. H. "The Sieve" (Sermon delivered January 1, 1874), Matthew 7:21. https://www.spurgeon.org/resource-library/sermons/the-sieve-2/#flipbook/, accessed March 2, 2021.

[56] Graham, Franklin. *Billy Graham in Quotes.* (Nashville: Thomas Nelson, 2011), 262.

[57] https://www.christianquotes.info/quotes-by-topic/quotes-about-persecution/, accessed February 17, 2021.

[58] Maclaren, Alexander. *Expositions of Holy Scriptures,* Vol. 6: Matthew 1–8. (Grand Rapids, MI: Baker Book House, 1977), 172.

[59] Foxe, John. *Foxe's Book of Martyrs.* "The First Persecution, Under Nero, A.D. 67."

[60] Ryle, J. C. *Expository Thoughts on the Gospels: Mark.* [Carlisle, PA: Banner of Truth, 1985], 329.

[61] Burton, Sir Richard Francis. https://www.wisesayings.com/spider-quotes/#ixzz6lmXb4Vuz, accessed February 7, 2021.

[62] Spurgeon, C. H. "A Word for the Persecuted" (Sermon delivered August 16, 1864), I Samuel 20:10. https://www.spurgeon.org/resource-library/sermons/a-word-for-the-persecuted/#flipbook/, accessed February 14, 2021.

[63] https://www.christianquotes.info/quotes-by-topic/quotes-about-persecution/, accessed February 17, 2021.

[64] Bunyan, John. *Grace Abounding.* (Evangelical Press, 2000), 143.

[65] Criswell, W. A. "Right Is Right Forever." Daily Word with W. A. Criswell, April 7.

[66] France, R.T. *Matthew: An Introduction and Commentary.* (Downers Grove, IL: InterVarsity Press, 1985), 116.

[67] Ironside, H. A. *Lectures on the Book of Revelation.* (Neptune, N. J.: Loizeaux Brothers, 1920), 71.

[68] Henry, M. *Matthew Henry's Commentary on the Whole Bible: Complete and Unabridged in One Volume.* (Peabody: Hendrickson, 1994), 1630.

[69] Barclay, W. (Ed.). *The Gospel of Matthew* (Vol. 1). (Philadelphia, PA: The Westminster John Knox Press, 1976), 378.

[70] Edwards, Jonathan. *Distinguishing Marks of a Work of the Spirit of God,* 1741. Modern language courtesy of Archie Parrish, The Spirit of Revival, (Crossway Books, 2000), 95.

[71] https://gracequotes.org/author-quote/henry-ward-beecher/, accessed April 21, 2021.

[72] Chafer, L. S. *Satan.* (New York: Gospel Publishing House, 1909), 80.

[73] Macaulay, J. C. *Obedient Unto Death: Devotional Studies in John's Gospel,* in MacDonald, W. *Believer's Bible Commentary: Old and New Testaments.* (A. Farstad, Ed.). (Nashville: Thomas Nelson, 1995), II:59.

[74] Spurgeon, C. H. *Morning and Evening,* November 17 (Evening).

[75] Swindoll, Chuck. *Paul: A Man of Grit & Grace.* (Nashville: W. Publishing Group, 2002), 4.

[76] Henry, M. *Matthew Henry's Commentary on the Whole Bible: Complete and Unabridged in One Volume.* (Peabody: Hendrickson, 1994), Acts 9:4.

[77] Yates, Kyle. *Preaching From the Prophets.* (Nashville: Broadman Press, 1942), 153–154.

[78] Calvin, John. *John Calvin's Commentaries,* Zechariah 2:8.

[79] MacArthur, J., Jr. (Ed.). *The MacArthur Study Bible* (electronic ed.). (Nashville, TN: Word Pub 1997), 1853.

[80] Henry, M. *Matthew Henry's Commentary on the Whole Bible: Complete and Unabridged in One Volume.* (Peabody: Hendrickson, 1994), 432.

[81] "Modern–Day Paul: "I Planned to Kill Him; Now I'm Prepared to Die for Jesus," https://www.opendoorsusa.org/christian-persecution/stories/modern-day-paul-i-planned-to-kill-him-now-im-prepared-to-die-for-jesus/, accessed March 17, 2021.

[82] Whitefield, George. *Whitefield's Sermons,* "Persecution, Every Christians's Lot." (Grand Rapids, MI: Christian Classics Ethereal Library).

[83] Graham, Billy. "The Cost of Discipleship" (Sermon delivered September 16, 1969. https://billygraham.org/audio/the-cost-of-discipleship/, accessed February 19, 2021.

[84] Bonhoeffer, Dietrich. The Cost of Discipleship. (New York: MacMillan Publishing Company, 1963).

[85] Pink, A. W. *An Exposition of Hebrews.* (Swengel, PA: Bible Truth Depot, 1954), 852.

[86] MacArthur, J., Jr. (Ed.). *The MacArthur Study Bible* (electronic ed.). (Nashville, TN: Word Pub, 1997), 1411.

[87] https://www.idlehearts.com/738774/carrying-the-cross-does-mean-following-in-jesus-footsteps-and-in-his, accessed April 6, 2021.

[88] Bonhoeffer, Dietrich. The Cost of Discipleship. (New York: MacMillan Publishing Company, 1963), 98–99.

[89] Courson, J. *Jon Courson's Application Commentary.* (Nashville, TN: Thomas Nelson, 2003), 130.

[90] Piper, John. *Jesus: The Only Way to God: Must You Hear the Gospel to Be Saved?* (Grand Rapids: Baker Books, 2010), 7–8.

[91] Yohannan, K. P. *Revolution in World Missions.* (Wills Point, TX: gfa books, a division of Gospel for Asia), 146.

[92] Pink, A. W. *An Exposition of Hebrews.* (Swengel, PA: Bible Truth Depot, 1954), 852.

[93] Exell, J. S. *The Biblical Illustrator: Matthew.* (Grand Rapids, MI: Baker Book House, 1952), 350.

[94] Ibid., 351.

[95] Graham, Billy. "What's the Cost of Following Jesus Christ?," audio-clip, August 2, 2017. https://billygraham.org/audio/billy-graham-whats-the-cost-of-following-jesus-christ/, accessed February 19, 2021.

[96] M'Cheyne. Robert Murray. https://gracequotes.org/topic/cross-bearing/, accessed March 5, 2021.

[97] Gordon, S. D. *Quiet Talks on Following the Christ,* Chapter: "The Pleading Call to Follow." https://www.gutenberg.org/files/18486/18486-h/18486-h.htm, accessed February 20, 2021.

[98] Bonhoeffer, Dietrich. The Cost of Discipleship. (New York: MacMillan Publishing Company, 1963), 91.

[99] *Notes on the Bible* by Albert Barnes [1834], Philippians 3:10.

[100] Finney, Charles. "The Blessedness of the Persecuted." *The Oberlin Evangelist,* September 15, 1858.

[101] https://www.christianquotes.info/quotes-by-topic/quotes-about-persecution/, accessed February 17, 2021.

[102] *Baptist Press.* Romanian Josef Tson recounts God's grace amid suffering, July 19, 2004.

[103] Criswell, W. A., Patterson, P., Clendenen, E. R., Akin, D. L., Chamberlin, M., Patterson, D. K., & Pogue, J. (Eds.). *Believer's Study Bible* (electronic ed.) (Nashville: Thomas Nelson, 1991), Colossians 1:24.

[104] Piper, John. "How Our Suffering Glorifies the Greatness of the Grace of God," sermon delivered at the Passion Conference, January 4, 2006. https://www.desiringgod.org/messages/how-our-suffering-glorifies-the-greatness-of-the-grace-of-god, accessed April 19, 2021.

[105] Minucius Felix, *The Octavius* 37, c. 200.

[106] Exell, J. S. *The Biblical Illustrator: Philippians–Colossians* (Vol. 1). (Grand Rapids, MI: Baker Book House, 1952), 75.

[107] Ibid., 74.

[108] https://www.christianquotes.info/quotes-by-topic/quotes-about-persecution/, accessed February 17, 2021.

[109] Quotes by Dwight L. Moody, http://www.jesus-is-savior.com, accessed January 29, 2014.

[110] Spence-Jones, H. D. M. (Ed.). *St. Matthew* (Vol. 1). (London; New York: Funk & Wagnalls Company, 1909), 151.

[111] Lust, J., E. Eynikel, and K. Hauspie. *A Greek-English Lexicon of the Septuagint: Revised Edition.* (Stuttgart: Deutsche Bibelgesellschaft, 2003).

112 Louw, J. P., and E. A. Nida. Greek-English Lexicon of the New Testament: Based on Semantic Domains (electronic ed. of the 2nd edition., Vol. 1). (New York: United Bible Societies, 1996), 302.

113 Henry, M. *Matthew Henry's Commentary on the Whole Bible: Complete and Unabridged in One Volume.* (Peabody: Hendrickson, 1994), 1630.

114 Howard, Tracy L. "Suffering in James 1:2–12." (Criswell Theological Review 1.1, 1986), 71–84.

115 Blomberg, C. *Matthew* (Vol. 22). (Nashville: Broadman & Holman Publishers, 1992), 101.

116 *John Calvin Commentaries,* Matthew 5:12.

117 Morris, L. *The Gospel According to Matthew.* (Grand Rapids, MI; Leicester, England: W.B. Eerdmans; Inter-Varsity Press, 1992), 101–102.

118 Newman, B. M., and P. C. Stine. *A Handbook on the Gospel of Matthew.* (New York: United Bible Societies, 1992), 116.

119 Henry, M. *Matthew Henry's Commentary on the Whole Bible: Complete and Unabridged in One Volume.* (Peabody: Hendrickson, 1994), 1630.

120 *Benson Commentary on the Old and New Testaments,* Matthew 5:11.

121 Pink, Arthur. "Identification of the Godly," March, 1945. https://gracegems.org/Pink/identification_of_the_godly.htm, accessed April 6, 2021.

122 Weber, S. K. *Matthew* (Vol. 1). (Nashville, TN: Broadman & Holman Publishers, 2000), 61.

123 MacArthur, J., Jr. (Ed.). *The MacArthur Study Bible* (electronic ed.). (Nashville, TN: Word Pub, 1997), 1708.

124 Johnson, Jeremiah. "Inviting Persecution." Blog, November 20, 2020. www.gty.org/library/blog/B151023, accessed April 19, 2021.

125 https://www.dailychristianquote.com/tag/persecution/, accessed February 5, 2021.

126 Watson, Thomas. *The Beatitudes: Concerning Persecution.* https://www.gracegems.org/Watson/beatitudes9.htm, accessed April 6, 2021.

127 Spurgeon, C. H. "The Sieve" (Sermon delivered January 1, 1874), Matthew 7:21. https://www.spurgeon.org/resource-library/sermons/the-sieve-2/#flipbook/, accessed March 2, 2021.

128 Spurgeon, C. H. "A Word for the Persecuted" (Sermon delivered August 16, 1864), I Samuel 20:10. https://www.spurgeon.org/resource-library/sermons/a-word-for-the-persecuted/#flipbook/, accessed February 14, 2021.

129 *Notes on the Bible* by Albert Barnes [1834], Matthew 5:12.

130 Thomas, I.D.E. *A Puritan Golden Treasury.* (Carlisle, PA: Banner of Truth, 2000), 53.

[131] Spurgeon, C. H. "A Word for the Persecuted" (Sermon delivered August 16, 1864), I Samuel 20:10. https://www.spurgeon.org/resource-library/sermons/a-word-for-the-persecuted/#flipbook/, accessed February 14, 2021.

[132] Morris, L. *The Gospel According to Matthew*. (Grand Rapids, MI; Leicester, England: W.B. Eerdmans; Inter-Varsity Press, 1992), 103.

[133] Newman, B. M., and P. C. Stine. *A Handbook on the Gospel of Matthew*. (New York: United Bible Societies, 1992), 116.

[134] Henry, M. *Matthew Henry's Commentary on the Whole Bible: Complete and Unabridged in One Volume*. (Peabody: Hendrickson, 1994), 1630.

[135] Jamieson, R., A. R. Fausset, and D. *Brown, Commentary Critical and Explanatory on the Whole Bible,* Vol. 2. (Oak Harbor, WA: Logos Research Systems, Inc., 1997), 556.

[136] Exell, J. S. *The Biblical Illustrator: Revelation*. (Grand Rapids, MI: Baker Book House, 1952), 2:10.

[137] The Crown of Righteousness (2 Timothy 4:8); The Incorruptible Crown (1 Corinthians 9:25); The Crown of Life (James 1:12); The Crown of Glory (1 Peter 5:2–4) and The Crown of Rejoicing (1 Thessalonians 2:19).

[138] Spence-Jones, H. D. M. (Ed.). *St. Luke* (Vol. 2). (London; New York: Funk & Wagnalls Company, 1909), 151.

[139] Henry, M. *Matthew Henry's Commentary on the Whole Bible: Complete and Unabridged in One Volume*. (Peabody: Hendrickson, 1994), 2471.

[140] Simeon, C. *Horae Homileticae:* James to Jude (Vol. 20). (London: Holdsworth and Ball, 1833), 24–25).

[141] Spurgeon, C. H. *Morning and Evening,* April 5 (Morning).

[142] Strauss, Richard L. "Hope for Suffering Saints (or: When the Giving Gets Tough!)," March 29, 1992. http://spiritualgold.org/transcripts/RW-05.html, accessed March 11, 2021.

[143] https://gracequotes.org/topic/martyrdom/, accessed March 17, 2021.

[144] Newman, John Henry. Parochial and Plain Sermons, Vol. II. (London, New York and Bombay: Longmans, Green and Company, 1898), 47.

[145] Pink, A. W. *An Exposition of Hebrews*. (Swengel, PA: Bible Truth Depot, 1954), 855.

[146] *Notes on the Bible* by Albert Barnes [1834], Matthew 10:17.

[147] Ibid., Acts 16:24.

[148] Ibid., Hebrews 11:37.

[149] Ibid.

[150] Pink, A. W. *An Exposition of Hebrews*. (Swengel, PA: Bible Truth Depot, 1954), 867.

151 Exell, J. S. *The Biblical Illustrator: Hebrews.* (Grand Rapids, MI: Baker Book House, 1952), 11:37–38.

152 Henry, M. *Matthew Henry's Commentary on the Whole Bible: Complete and Unabridged in One Volume.* (Peabody: Hendrickson, 1994), Hebrews 11:37–38.

153 Pink, A. W. *An Exposition of Hebrews.* (Swengel, PA: Bible Truth Depot, 1954), 866.

154 Ibid.

155 Clarke, Adam. *Commentary on the Bible.* (1831), Hebrews 11:37.

156 Simeon, C. *Horae Homileticae: 2 Timothy to Hebrews* (Vol. 19). (London: Holdsworth and Ball, 1833), 438.

157 Henry, M. *Matthew Henry's Commentary on the Whole Bible: Complete and Unabridged in One Volume.* (Peabody: Hendrickson, 1994), 1630.

158 Barclay, W. (Ed.). *The Gospel of Matthew* (Vol. 1). (Philadelphia, PA: The Westminster John Knox Press, 1976), 112.

159 Exell, J. S. *The Biblical Illustrator: Hebrews* (Vol. 2). (Grand Rapids, MI: Baker Book House, 1952), 424.

160 Ibid.

161 "Brazen Bull." https://en.wikipedia.org/wiki/Brazen_bull, accessed February 19, 2021.

162 Exell, J. S. *The Biblical Illustrator: Hebrews* (Vol. 2). (Grand Rapids, MI: Baker Book House, 1952), 424.

163 *The Complete Works of Richard Sibbes.* (Edinburgh: James Nichol, 1862), 168.

164 Louw, J. P., and E. A. Nida. Greek-English Lexicon of the New Testament: Based on Semantic Domains (electronic ed. of the 2nd edition., Vol. 1). (New York: United Bible Societies, 1996), 755.

165 Pink, Arthur. "Identification of the Godly," March, 1945. https://gracegems. org/Pink/identification_of_the_godly.htm, accessed April 6, 2021.

166 Barnes Notes on the Bible, Matthew 10:16.

167 Nolland, J. *The Gospel of Matthew: A Commentary on the Greek Text.* (Grand Rapids, MI; Carlisle: W.B. Eerdmans; Paternoster Press, 2005), 423.

168 Morris, L. *The Gospel According to Matthew.* (Grand Rapids, MI; Leicester, England: W.B. Eerdmans; Inter-Varsity Press, 1992), 253.

169 Simeon, C. *Horae Homileticae: Matthew* (Vol. 11). (London: Holdsworth and Ball, 1832–1863), 319.

170 https://gracequotes.org/topic/spiritual-warfare-enemies-satan/, accessed March 20, 2021.

[171] Morris, L. *The Gospel According to Matthew.* (Grand Rapids, MI; Leicester, England: W.B. Eerdmans; Inter-Varsity Press, 1992), 253.

[172] Exell, J. S. *The Biblical Illustrator: Matthew.* (Grand Rapids, MI: Baker Book House, 1952), 180.

[173] Carson, D. A. *The Expositor's Bible Commentary: Matthew, Mark, Luke* (Vol. 8). F. E. Gaebelein (Ed.). (Grand Rapids: Zondervan Publishing House, 1984), 247.

[174] Weber, S. K. *Matthew* (Vol. 1). (Nashville, TN: Broadman & Holman Publishers, 2000), 144.

[175] *Notes on the Bible* by Albert Barnes [1834], Matthew 10:28.

[176] Henry, M. *Matthew Henry's Commentary on the Whole Bible: Complete and Unabridged in One Volume.* (Peabody: Hendrickson, 1994), 1661.

[177] Campbell, I. D. *Opening Up Matthew.* (Leominster: Day One Publications, 2008), 65.

[178] https://www.tyndale.com/sites/readthearc/true-stories-of-the-persecuted-church-around-the-world/, accessed March 12, 2021.

[179] https://www.azquotes.com/quote/1414713, accessed May 7, 2021.

[180] Tertullian. *De Fuga in Persecutione, 14.*

[181] Foxe, John. *Foxe's Christian Martyrs: The Powerful Abridged Classic.* (Uhrichsville, OH: Barbour Books, 2005), 44.

[182] https://www.brainyquote.com/quotes/mark_twain_138540, accessed March 5, 2021.

[183] https://www.christianquotes.info/quotes-by-topic/quotes-about-courage/, accessed February 5, 2021.

[184] Spence-Jones, H. D. M. (Ed.). *Proverbs.* (London; New York: Funk & Wagnalls Company, 1909), 533.

[185] Pink, A. W. *An Exposition of Hebrews.* (Swengel, PA: Bible Truth Depot, 1954), 853.

[186] https://www.brainyquote.com/quotes/billy_graham_113622, accessed July 14, 2021.

[187] Hayford, J. W. (Ed.). (1997). Spirit filled life study Bible (electronic ed., Heb 1:7). Nashville, TN: Thomas Nelson.

[188] Ibid.

[189] Spurgeon, C.H. *Morning and Evening,* October 3.

[190] Exell, J. S. *The Biblical Illustrator: Hebrews* (Vol. 1). (Grand Rapids, MI: Baker Book House, 1952), 64.

[191] Graham, Billi, Angels, God's Secret Agents, Doubleday & Company, Inc., Garden City, NY, 1975, p. 2-3.

[192] Ibid., back cover.

[193] www.whatchristianswanttoknow.com/bible-verses-about-worry-20-comforting-scripture-quotes, accessed September 4, 2017.

[194] Bonhoeffer, Dietrich. *The Cost of Discipleship*. (New York: MacMillan Publishing Company, 1963), 242.

[195] Contributed by Dr. Nina Gunter who got it from veteran missionary Louise Robinson Chapman (Africa: 1920–1940).

[196] Tozer, A. W. *The Works of A. W. Tozer*.

[197] Spurgeon, C. H. "The War of Truth" (January 11, 1857), *New Park Street Pulpit*, Volume 3.

[198] Barnes, Albert. *Notes on the Bible*. (1834), Romans 12:14.

[199] Spurgeon, C. H. "A Word for the Persecuted" (Sermon delivered August 16, 1864), I Samuel 20:10. https://www.spurgeon.org/resource-library/sermons/a-word-for-the-persecuted/#flipbook/, accessed February 14, 2021.

[200] Gill, John. *Exposition of the Entire Bible*. (1746–63), Matthew 5:44.

[201] https://www.azquotes.com/author/27034-Justin_Martyr, accessed May 7, 2021.

[202] MacArthur, J., Jr. (Ed.). *The MacArthur Study Bible* (electronic ed.). (Nashville, TN: Word Pub, 1997), 913.

[203] Spence-Jones, H. D. M. (Ed.). *Proverbs*. (London; New York: Funk & Wagnalls Company, 1909), 484.

[204] Henry, M. *Matthew Henry's Commentary on the Whole Bible: Complete and Unabridged in One Volume*. (Peabody: Hendrickson, 1994), 1012.

[205] Chambers, Oswald. *My Utmost for His Highest*, July 14.

[206] Bonhoeffer, Dietrich. *The Cost of Discipleship*. (New York: Collier Books, 1963), 164.

[207] Crockett, Kent. *The 911 Handbook*. (Peabody, MA: Hendrickson Publishers, 2003), 43.

[208] "Persecution and the Gospel," DVD. Billy Graham Evangelistic Association, 2020.

[209] Edwards, Jonathan. (Ed. by Wilson Kimnach, Kenneth P. Minkema, and Douglas Sweeney). *The Sermons of Jonathan Edwards: A Reader*, "The Pleasantness of Religion". (New Haven: Yale University Press, 1999), 20.

[210] https://www.brainyquote.com/quotes/corrie_ten_boom_381187.

[211] Courson, J. *Jon Courson's Application Commentary*. (Nashville, TN: Thomas Nelson, 2003), 1630.

[212] MacArthur, John. "Answering the Hard Questions About Forgiveness." http://www.gty.org, accessed July 30, 2014.

[213] *Notes on the Bible* by Albert Barnes [1834], Matthew 5:11.

[214] Ibid., 1 Peter 2:19.

[215] https://www.azquotes.com/quote/1366382, accessed May 7, 2021.

[216] Spurgeon, C. H. "God's People in the Furnace" (Sermon delivered August 12, 1885). *New Park Street Pulpit,* Volume 1.

[217] Exell, J. S. *The Biblical Illustrator: Revelation.* (Grand Rapids, MI: Baker Book House, 1952), 2:10.

[218] Spurgeon, C. H. "A Word for the Persecuted" (Sermon delivered August 16, 1864), I Samuel 20:10. https://www.spurgeon.org/resource-library/sermons/a-word-for-the-persecuted/#flipbook/, accessed February 14, 2021.

[219] Barclay, W. (Ed.). *The Gospel of Matthew* (Vol. 1). (Philadelphia, PA: The Westminster John Knox Press, 1976), 117.

[220] Barnes Notes on the Bible, Mark 10:30.

[221] Ironside, H. A. *Ironside's Notes on Selected Books.* "Commentary on Isaiah 40:4." https://www.studylight.org/commentaries/isn/isaiah-40.html. 1914.

[222] Spurgeon, C. H. "A Word for the Persecuted" (Sermon delivered August 16, 1864), I Samuel 20:10. https://www.spurgeon.org/resource-library/sermons/a-word-for-the-persecuted/#flipbook/, accessed February 14, 2021.

[223] Barclay, W. (Ed.). *The Daily Study Bible Series.* The Revelation of John: Volume 2. (Philadelphia:The Westminster John Knox Press, 1976), 83

[224] Spurgeon, C. H. *The Treasury of David,* Psalm 7:11.

[225] Lee, R. G. "Payday, Someday." http://baptiststudiesonline.com/wp-content/uploads/2008/08/payday-someday.pdf, accessed March 13, 2021.

[226] Barnes Notes on the Bible, Acts 5:39.

[227] Ibid.

[228] Ibid., Mark 10:30.

[229] Plumer, W. S. Studies in the Book of Psalms: Being a Critical and Expository Commentary, with Doctrinal and Practical Remarks on the Entire Psalter. (Philadelphia; Edinburgh: J. B. Lippincott Company; A & C Black, 1872), 1109.

[230] Piper, John. "How Our Suffering Glorifies the Greatness of the Grace of God" (sermon delivered January 4, 2006). https://www.desiringgod.org/messages/how-our-suffering-glorifies-the-greatness-of-the-grace-of-god, accessed April 19, 2021.

[231] Henry, M. *Matthew Henry's Commentary on the Whole Bible: Complete and Unabridged in One Volume.* (Peabody: Hendrickson, 1994), 2323.

[232] https://www.christianquotes.info/quotes-by-topic/quotes-about-satan/, accessed March 19, 2021.

[233] Spurgeon, C. H. "A Word for the Persecuted" (Sermon delivered August 16, 1864), I Samuel 20:10. https://www.spurgeon.org/resource-library/sermons/a-word-for-the-persecuted/#flipbook/, accessed February 14, 2021.

[234] Clarke, Adam. *Commentary on the Bible*. (1831), Matthew 16:18.

[235] Spence-Jones, H. D. M. (Ed.). *St. Matthew* (Vol. 2). (London; New York: Funk & Wagnalls Company, 1909), 136.

[236] *Notes on the Bible* by Albert Barnes [1834], Revelation 6:9.

[237] MacDonald, W. *Believer's Bible Commentary: Old and New Testaments*. (A. Farstad, Ed.) (Nashville: Thomas Nelson, 1995), 1239.

[238] Graham, Franklin. *Billy Graham in Quotes*. (Nashville: Thomas Nelson, 2011), 260.

[239] Criswell, W. A. *What To Do Until Jesus Comes Back*. (Nashville: Broadman Press, 1975), 14.

[240] https://www.christianitytoday.com/history/quotes/, accessed March 17, 2021.

[241] https://gracequotes.org/author-quote/henry-ward-beecher/, accessed April 21, 2021.

[242] Spurgeon, C. H. *Morning and Evening*, April 5 (Morning).

[243] Exell, J. S. *The Biblical Illustrator: Philippians–Colossians* (Vol. 1). (Grand Rapids, MI: Baker Book House, 1952), 75.

[244] https://www.goodreads.com/quotes/tag/persecution?page=5, accessed March 17, 2021.

[245] https://www.azquotes.com/quote/1402590, accessed May 7, 2021.

[246] Exell, J. S. *The Biblical Illustrator: Jude*. (Grand Rapids, MI: Baker Book House, 1952), 13.

[247] Spurgeon, C. H. *Exploring the Mind and Heart of the Prince of Preachers* (Kerry James Allen, Ed.). (Oswego, Ill: Fox River Press, 2005), 30.

[248] Lewis, C. S. *Mere Christianity*, 51.

[249] Lutzer, Erwin and David Jeremiah. *We Will Not Be Silenced*. (Eugene, Oregon: Harvest House Publishers, 2020), 247.

[250] *The Criswell Study Bible*, Jude 3.

[251] Zacharias, Ravi. *Can a Man Live without God?* (Nashville: Word Publishing Group, 1994), ix–x.

[252] MacArthur, J., Jr. (Ed.). *The MacArthur Study Bible* (electronic ed.). (Nashville, TN: Word Pub, 1997), 1985.

[253] Ibid.

[254] https://www.dailychristianquote.com/tag/persecution/, accessed March 17, 2021.

[255] Gordon, S. D. https://www.christianquotes.info/quotes-by-topic/quotes-about-satan/, accessed March 20, 2021.

[256] When You Don't Fit In Because of Your Faith: An Exposition of 1 Peter. Voice.dts.edu, Dallas Theological Seminary, July 7, 2006. Accessed April 17, 2021.

[257] O'Brien, P. T. *The Epistle to the Philippians: A Commentary on the Greek Text.* (Grand Rapids, MI: Eerdmans, 1991), 520.

[258] Exell, J. S. *The Biblical Illustrator: Philippians–Colossians, Vol. 1.* (New York; Chicago; Toronto; London; Edinburgh: Fleming H. Revell Company), 347.

[259] Cowman, L. B. *Streams in the Desert.* (Grand Rapids: Zondervan, 1997), January 5.

[260] Spurgeon, C. H. *Morning and Evening,* August 5 (Morning).

[261] Macdonald, J. A. *The Pulpit Commentary.* "The Blessedness of Persecution" (Sermon), Matthew 5:10–12.

[262] *Enduring Word.* "Hebrews 12—Reasons to Endure Discouraging Times." https://enduringword.com/bible-commentary/hebrews-12/, accessed March 24, 2020.

[263] Wuest, K. S. *Wuest's Word Studies from the Greek New Testament for the English Reader.* (Grand Rapids: Eerdmans, 1997), Heb 12:1.

[264] Hagner, Donald A. *New International Biblical Commentary.* (Carlisle, PA: Hendrickson Publishers, 1990), 211.

[265] Hacking, P. H. *Opening up Hebrews.* (Leominster: Day One Publications, 2006), 82.

[266] Spurgeon, C. H. *Beside Still Waters: Words of Comfort for the Soul.* (Nashville: Thomas Nelson, 1999), 2.

[267] Whitefield, George. *The Works of the Reverend George Whitefield: Containing All His Sermons and Tracts Which Have Been Already Published.*

[268] https://www.rylequotes.org/quotes/category/persecution, accessed February 27, 2021.

[269] *John Calvin Commentaries,* Matthew 5:10–11.

[270] Spurgeon, C. H. "A Word for the Persecuted" (Sermon delivered August 16, 1864), I Samuel 20:10. https://www.spurgeon.org/resource-library/sermons/a-word-for-the-persecuted/#flipbook/, accessed February 14, 2021.

[271] MacArthur, John. *Follow Me.* (Nashville, TN: Countryman, 2004), 72.

[272] Calvin, John. *John Calvin's Commentaries,* Matthew 5:10.

[273] Graham, Billy. *Decision Magazine,* "Prepare for Persecution: A Message from Billy Graham," (adapted), November 9, 2015.

274 Wilkerson, David. *Bring Your Loved Ones to Christ.* (New Jersey: Fleming Revell Company, 1979), 116.

275 https://www.goodreads.com/author/quotes/10120864.R_A_Torrey, accessed February 20, 2021.

276 Barnes Notes on the Bible, Ephesians 6:14.

277 Exell, J. S. *The Biblical Illustrator: Hebrews* (Vol. 2). (Grand Rapids, MI: Baker Book House, 1952), 457.

278 Carroll, B. H. *An Interpretation of the English Bible: The Pastoral Epistles,* 332–333.

279 Spurgeon, C. H. *Faith's Checkbook,* December 16.

280 Yates, Kyle. *Preaching From the Prophets.* (Nashville: Broadman Press, 1942), 168.

281 Thomas, R. L. *New American Standard Hebrew-Aramaic and Greek Dictionaries* (updated edition). (Anaheim: Foundation Publications, Inc. 1998).

282 Graham, Billy. *Decision Magazine,* "Prepare for Persecution: A Message from Billy Graham," November 9, 2015.

283 Lloyd-Jones, Martyn. *The Christian Soldier.* (Grand Rapids: Baker, 1977), 179.

284 Morgan, G. Campbell. *The Westminster Pulpit.* (Grand Rapids: Baker Books, 2006), Volume IX, 310–311.

285 *Our Daily Bread,* Thursday, February 21.

286 Greg Laurie. "Devotion: For Righteousness' Sake," March 01, 2019. https://harvest.org/resources/devotion/for-righteousness-sake-2019/, accessed April 10, 2021.

287 Barclay, W. (Ed.). *The Gospel of Matthew* (Vol. 1). (Philadelphia, PA: The Westminster John Knox Press, 1976), 116.

288 Morris, L. *The Gospel According to Matthew.* (Grand Rapids, MI; Leicester, England: W.B. Eerdmans; Inter-Varsity Press, 1992), 257.

289 Henry, M. and T. Scott. *Matthew Henry's Concise Commentary.* (Oak Harbor, WA: Logos Research Systems, 1997), Mt. 10:16.

290 Morris, L. *The Gospel According to Matthew.* (Grand Rapids, MI; Leicester, England: W.B. Eerdmans; Inter-Varsity Press, 1992), 152.

291 Blomberg, C. *Matthew* (Vol. 22). (Nashville: Broadman & Holman Publishers, 1992), 176.

292 Spence-Jones, H. D. M. (Ed.). *St. Matthew* (Vol. 1). (London; New York: Funk & Wagnalls Company, 1909), 412.

293 See Ignatius letter to the Roman Church (Rom. 1.2; 6.3; 7.2).

294 Ibid., (Rom. 1.2).

295 Ibid., (Rom. 4).

[296] Ibid., (Rom. 6.1–3).

[297] Tertullian. *De Fuga in Persecutione,* 14.

[298] Spurgeon, C. H. *Morning and Evening,* May 26 (Evening).

[299] Bad Urach Statement, 2010. "Towards an Evangelical Theology of Suffering, Persecution and Martyrdom for the Global Church in Mission," in *Suffering, Persecution and Martyrdom: Theological Reflections,* (edited by Sauer, C. and R. Howell), Religious Freedom Series, 2. (Johannesburg; Bonn: AcadSA; VKW), 27–106.

[300] Sauer, Christof. "To Flee or Not to Flee": Responses to Persecution and the Issue of Relocation. *Missionalia* (Online), vol. 41, n.1. Pretoria, Aug. 2013.

[301] Thomas Schirrmacher. An Evangelical Code of Ethics for Christian Mission. http://www.worldevangelicals.org/WEA_Ethics_Code_draft_2010.pdf, accessed April 14, 2021.

[302] Rogers, Adrian. "Preparing for the Coming Persecution." https://www.oneplace.com/ministries/love-worth-finding/read/articles/preparing-for-the-coming-persecution-17488.html, accessed February 9, 2021.

[303] Graham, Franklin. *Billy Graham in Quotes.* (Nashville: Thomas Nelson, 2011), 74.

[304] Criswell, W. A. *Daily Word,* "The Cost of Standing for Truth," August 2, 2021.

[305] https://www.studylight.org/commentary/1-samuel/20-30.html, accessed August 2, 2021.

[306] Mohler, Albert. "Pivoting to Surrender" (article). https://albertmohler.com/2021/03/04/pivoting-to-surrender-a-warning-for-all-christians, accessed April 5, 2021.

[307] The Expositor's Greek Testament – Nicoll, Matthew 5:10-11.

[308] Barclay, W. (Ed.). *The Letters to the Galatians and Ephesians.* (Philadelphia, PA: The Westminster John Knox Press, 1976), 57.

[309] Exell, J. S. *The Biblical Illustrator: Galations.* (Grand Rapids, MI: Baker Book House, 1952), 550.

[310] Ibid.

[311] https://www.azquotes.com/quote/662633, accessed May 9, 2021.

[312] MacArthur, J., Jr. (Ed.). *The MacArthur Study Bible* (electronic ed.). (Nashville, TN: Word Pub, 1997), 1783.

[313] *Notes on the Bible* by Albert Barnes [1834], 2 Corinthians 12:10.

[314] Spurgeon, C. H. "A Word for the Persecuted" (Sermon delivered August 16, 1864), I Samuel 20:10. https://www.spurgeon.org/resource-library/sermons/a-word-for-the-persecuted/#flipbook/, accessed February 14, 2021.

[315] Redpath, Alan. *The Price and Privilege of Discipleship,* 1955.

316 Henry, M. *Matthew Henry's Commentary on the Whole Bible: Complete and Unabridged in One Volume*. (Peabody: Hendrickson, 1994), 2291.

317 Spence-Jones, H. D. M. (Ed.). *2 Thessalonians*. (London; New York: Funk & Wagnalls Company, 1909), 10–11.

318 Exell, J. S. *The Biblical Illustrator: Galations*. (Grand Rapids, MI: Baker Book House, 1952), Acts 9:4.

319 https://www.inspiringquotes.us/quotes/BmKy_nbF6JjRm, accessed May 9, 2021.

320 Harris, M. J. *The Second Epistle to the Corinthians: A Commentary on the Greek Text*. (Grand Rapids, MI; Milton Keynes, UK: W.B. Eerdmans Pub. Co.; Paternoster Press, 2005), 862.

321 Henry, M. *Matthew Henry's Commentary on the Whole Bible: Complete and Unabridged in One Volume*. (Peabody: Hendrickson, 1994), 2291.

322 Spurgeon, C. H. *Morning and Evening,* May 26 (Evening).

323 Henry, M. *Matthew Henry's Commentary on the Whole Bible: Complete and Unabridged in One Volume*. (Peabody: Hendrickson, 1994), 1740.

324 Utley, R. J. *The First Christian Primer: Matthew* (Vol. 9). (Marshall, TX: Bible Lessons International, 2000), 198

325 MacArthur, J., Jr. (Ed.). *The MacArthur Study Bible* (electronic ed.). (Nashville, TN: Word Pub, 1997), 1439.

326 MacDonald, *W. Believer's Bible Commentary: Old and New Testaments*. (A. Farstad, Ed.) (Nashville: Thomas Nelson, 1995), 1294.

327 Morris, L. *The Gospel According to Matthew*. (Grand Rapids, MI; Leicester, England: W.B. Eerdmans; Inter-Varsity Press, 1992), 601.

328 Ibid., 256.

329 Spurgeon, C. H. "A Word for the Persecuted" (Sermon delivered August 16, 1864), 1 Samuel 20:10. https://www.spurgeon.org/resource-library/sermons/a-word-for-the-persecuted/#flipbook/, accessed February 14, 2021.

330 Churchill, Winston. *The Best of Winston Churchill's Speeches*. "Never Give In!" http://www.goodreads.com, accessed January 23, 2014.

331 Calvin, John. *John Calvin's Commentaries,* Matthew 5:12.

332 https://www.christianquotes.info/quotes-by-topic/quotes-about-persecution/, accessed February 5, 2021.

333 https://gracequotes.org/topic/spiritual-warfare-enemies-satan/, accessed March 20, 2021.

334 Exell, J. S. *The Biblical Illustrator: Matthew*. (Grand Rapids, MI: Baker Book House, 1952), 5:11.

335 Clarke, Adam. *Commentary on the Bible*. (1831), Matthew 5:110.

[336] Hagner, D. A. *Matthew 1–13* (Vol. 33A). (Dallas: Word, Incorporated, 1993), 91.

[337] Weber, S. K. *Matthew* (Vol. 1). (Nashville, TN: Broadman & Holman Publishers, 2000), 60.

[338] MacDonald, W. *Believer's Bible Commentary: Old and New Testaments.* (A. Farstad, Ed.) (Nashville: Thomas Nelson, 1995), 1711.

[339] https://www.christianquotes.info/quotes-by-topic/quotes-about-persecution/, accessed February 17, 2021.

[340] *Nicene and Post-Nicene Fathers, First Series,* Vol. 10. Edited by Philip Schaff. (Buffalo, NY: Christian Literature Publishing Co., 1888.)

[341] Morris, L. *The Gospel According to Matthew.* (Grand Rapids, MI; Leicester, England: W.B. Eerdmans; Inter-Varsity Press, 1992), 102.

[342] *The Highest Good/The Shadow of an Agony.* (Grand Rapids: Discovery House, 1965), Psalm 124.

[343] Courson, J. *Jon Courson's Application Commentary.* (Nashville, TN: Thomas Nelson, 2003), 27.

[344] Hughes, Kent. *Luke,* Vol. 1, "The Sermon on the Level." (Wheaton: Crossway Books, 1998), 221.

[345] Redpath, Alan. "The Price and Privilege of Discipleship," sermon delivered September 11, 1955, at the Moody Church, Chicago, Ill.

[346] Simeon, C. *Horae Homileticae:* Matthew (Vol. 11). (London: Holdsworth and Ball, 1832–1863), 79.

[347] Ross, Allen. *The Expositor's Bible Commentary: Proverbs-Isaiah.* (Longman, T. and D. Garland, Ed.) (Grand Rapids: Zondervan, 2008), 163.

[348] https://www.christianquotes.info/quotes-by-topic/quotes-about-wisdom/, accessed March 14, 2021.

[349] Ravenhill, Leonard. "Suffering—The Marks of God's Approval."

[350] https://www.brainyquote.com/quotes/gilbert_k_chesterton_163172, accessed May 10, 2021.

[351] Lee, Robert G., "By Christ Compelled" in the Robert G. Lee Sermonic Library. (Orlando, FL, Christ for the World Publishers, 1981), 32.

[352] https://gracequotes.org/author-quote/henry-ward-beecher/, accessed April 21, 2021.

[353] https://quotefancy.com/quote/1446577/Aiden-Wilson-Tozer-I-claim-the-holy-right-to-disappoint-men-in-order-to-avoid, accessed April 5, 2021.

[354] *A. W. Tozer Bible.* (2012), 222.

[355] Watson, Thomas. *The Beatitudes: Concerning Persecution.* https://www.gracegems.org/Watson/beatitudes9.htm, accessed April 6, 2021.

[356] Truett, George W. *Baptist Standard*, "Religious Liberty". August 22, 2016. https://www.baptiststandard.com/opinion/other-opinions/george-w-truett-on-religious-liberty/, accessed February 25, 2021.

[357] https://www.christianquotes.info/quotes-by-topic/quotes-about-satan/, accessed March 20, 2021.

[358] Rosscup, *How to Preach Biblically*, 70.

[359] https://quotefancy.com/quote/45965/Martin-Luther-I-have-held-many-things-in-my-hands-and-I-have-lost-them-all-but-whatever-I, accessed May 7, 2021.

[360] Henry, M. and T. Scott. *Matthew Henry's Concise Commentary.* (Oak Harbor, WA: Logos Research Systems, 1997), Mt. 16:24.

[361] From the First Apology of Justin Martyr (AD 150).

[362] Spurgeon, C. H. "A Word for the Persecuted" (Sermon delivered August 16, 1864), I Samuel 20:10. https://www.spurgeon.org/resource-library/sermons/a-word-for-the-persecuted/#flipbook/, accessed February 14, 2021.

[363] Spurgeon, C. H. "A Word for the Persecuted" (Sermon delivered August 16, 1864), I Samuel 20:10. https://www.spurgeon.org/resource-library/sermons/a-word-for-the-persecuted/#flipbook/, accessed February 14, 2021.

[364] https://www.christianquotes.info/quotes-by-topic/quotes-about-persecution/, accessed February 17, 2021.

[365] Thomas, I.D.E. *A Puritan Golden Treasury.* (Carlisle, PA: Banner of Truth, 2000), 208.

[366] Packer, J. I. *Affirming the Apostle's Creed.* (Wheaton, ILL: Crossway Books, 2008), 108.

[367] https://www.goodreads.com/quotes/657155-if-i-profess-with-the-loudest-voice-and-clearest-exposition, accessed February 21, 2021.

[368] https://www.rylequotes.org/quotes/category/persecution, accessed February 27, 2021.

[369] https://faithunlocked.wordpress.com/2014/08/09/quotes-on-persecution/, accessed March 17, 2021.

[370] Simeon, C. *Horae Homileticae:* Matthew (Vol. 11). (London: Holdsworth and Ball, 1832–1863), 79.

[371] Finney, Charles. *The Oberlin Evangelist.* "The Blessedness of the Persecuted," September 15, 1858.

[372] Graham, Billy. *Decision Magazine,* "Prepare for Persecution: A Message from Billy Graham," November 9, 2015.

[373] Foxe, John. *Book of Marytrs,* Chapter 1. https://bibletruthpublishers.com/book-of-martyrs-chapter-1/john-foxe/foxes-book-of-martyrs/john-foxe/la89803, accessed February 17, 2021.

[374] Gill, John. *Exposition of the Entire Bible.* (1746–63), Matthew 16:24.

[375] Studd, Mrs. C. T. *The Sword of the Lord,* "Men on Fire." (Murfreesboro, TN: Sword of the Lord, Nov.5, 2004), 4.

[376] https://www.ccel.org/ccel/edwards/affections.iii.html, accessed April 6, 2021.

[377] Bonhoeffer, Dietrich. The Cost of Discipleship. (New York: MacMillan Publishing Company, 1963).

[378] Poland, Larry W. *The Coming Persecution.* (San Bernardino, California: Here's Life Publishers, 1990), 41.

[379] https://quotefancy.com/quote/791951, accessed May 9, 2021.

[380] Limbaugh, David. *Persecution: How Liberals Are Waging War Against Christians.* (Regnery Publishing, August 1, 2003), Introduction.

[381] MacArthur, J., Jr. (Ed.). *The MacArthur Study Bible* (electronic ed.). (Nashville, TN: Word Pub, 1997), 1438.

[382] Lindsey, Hal. *Planet Earth—2000 A.D.* (Palos Verdes, California: Western Front, LTD., 1994), 279.

[383] Redpath, Alan. "The Price and Privilege of Discipleship," sermon delivered September 11, 1955, at the Moody Church, Chicago, Ill.

[384] "A Closer Look at How Religious Restrictions Have Risen Around the World," July 15, 2019. https://www.pewforum.org/2019/07/15/a-closer-look-at-how-religious-restrictions-have-risen-around-the-world/, accessed April 15, 2021.

[385] Jackson, Griffin Paul. *Christianity Today,* "No Matter Where You Are, Religious Freedom Is Getting Worse," July 15, 2019. https://www.christianitytoday.com/news/2019/july/religious-freedom-getting-worse-pew-ministerial.html, accessed March 25, 2021.

[386] "Christian Persecution." https://www.churchinneed.org/christian-persecution/, accessed February 18, 2021.

[387] Persecuted for Christ! https://savethepersecutedchristians.org/persecution-by-the-numbers/, accessed February 11, 2021.

[388] Graham, Franklin. "Persecution on an Unprecedented Scale," June 1, 2017. https://billygraham.org/story/franklin-graham-persecution-on-an-unprecedented-scale/, accessed April 22, 2021.

[389] "World of Faith under Siege; Threats Are Growing." *The Catholic Register,* July 24, 2019. https://angelusnews.com/news/life-family/world-of-faith-under-siege-with-threats-multiplying-daily-says-smith/, accessed April 17, 2021.

390 Graham, Franklin. *Billy Graham in Quotes.* (Nashville: Thomas Nelson, 2011), 261.

391 Lowry, Lindy. "11 of the Top Persecutors Around the World Today," July 10, 2019. https://www.opendoorsusa.org/christian-persecution/stories/11-of-the-top-persecutors-around-the-world-today/, accessed March 19, 2021.

392 Jackson, Griffin Paul. *Christianity Today,* "No Matter Where You Are, Religious Freedom Is Getting Worse," July 15, 2019. https://www.christianitytoday.com/news/2019/july/religious-freedom-getting-worse-pew-ministerial.html, accessed March 25, 2021.

393 Schirrmacher, Thomas. *The Persecution of Christians Concerns Us All.* (Eugene: OR, Wipf & Stock Publishers, 2018), 14.

394 Louw, J. P., and E. A. Nida. Greek-English Lexicon of the New Testament: Based on Semantic Domains (electronic ed. of the 2nd edition., Vol. 1). (New York: United Bible Societies, 1996), 347.

395 Arndt, W., F. W. Danker, W. Bauer, and F. W. Gingrich. *A Greek-English Lexicon of the New Testament and Other Early Christian Literature,* (3rd ed.). (Chicago: University of Chicago Press, 2000), 652.

396 Swanson, J. *Dictionary of Biblical Languages with Semantic Domains: Greek* (New Testament) (electronic ed.). (Oak Harbor: Logos Research Systems, Inc., 1997).

397 "Persecution and the Gospel," DVD. Billy Graham Evangelistic Association, 2020. Excellent resource to awaken the saint to the reality of the present horrific persecution of Christians around the world.

398 Exell, J. S. *The Biblical Illustrator: Hebrews* (Vol. 2). (Grand Rapids, MI: Baker Book House, 1952), 597.

399 Harnack, Adolf. *The Mission and Expansion of Christianity in the First Three Centuries,* Vol. 1. (New York: G.P. Putnam's Son, 1908), 163.

400 Wurmbrand, Richard. *Tortured for Christ.*

401 *Vincent's Word Studies,* Hebrews 11:33.

402 Zodhiates, S. *The Complete Word Study Dictionary: New Testament* (electronic ed.). (Chattanooga, TN: AMG Publishers, 2000).

403 *Matthew Poole's Commentary,* Hebrews 11:33.

404 Johnson, S. Lewis. *Some Imperatives and the Great Indicative: Hebrews.* https://sljinstitute.net/general-epistles/hebrews/some-imperatives-and-the-great-indicative-hebrews/, accessed May 7, 2021.

405 Ibid.

406 Lovell, Ann. *SBC News,* Prayer, "The Persecuted Church." (International Mission Board), May 26, 2020.

407 https://www.christianquotes.info/quotes-by-topic/quotes-about-persecution/, accessed February 17, 2021.

408 https://www.opendoorsusa.org/about-us/history/brother-andrews-story/, accessed March 19, 2021.

409 Towns, Emily. "Four Ways to Pray for the Persecuted Church." October 22, 2018. https://worldhelp.net/4-ways-to-pray-for-the-persecuted-church/, accessed May 7, 2021.

410 https://www.dailychristianquote.com/tag/persecution/, accessed February 5, 2021.

411 https://www.christianquotes.info/quotes-by-topic/quotes-about-persecution/, accessed February 17, 2021.

412 Exell, J. S. *The Biblical Illustrator: Hebrews* (Vol. 2). (Grand Rapids, MI: Baker Book House, 1952), 428.

413 Inspired and adapted from W. A. Criswell's sermon "The Christian Martyr." https://wacriswell.com/sermons/1976/the-christian-martyr1/, accessed February 17, 2021.

414 Pink, A. W. *An Exposition of Hebrews.* (Swengel, PA: Bible Truth Depot, 1954), 854.

415 *Notes on the Bible* by Albert Barnes [1834], Hebrews 11:38.

416 Farrar, F. W. *The Epistle of Paul the Apostle to the Hebrews, With Notes and Introduction.* (Cambridge: Cambridge University Press, 1893), 150.

417 Exell, J. S. *The Biblical Illustrator: Hebrews* (Vol. 2). (Grand Rapids, MI: Baker Book House, 1952), 430.

418 Henry, M. and T. Scott. *Matthew Henry's Concise Commentary.* (Oak Harbor, WA: Logos Research Systems, 1997), Heb. 11:32.

419 Barclay, W. (Ed.). *The Gospel of Matthew* (Vol. 1). (Philadelphia, PA: The Westminster John Knox Press, 1976), 117.

420 https://www.heartlight.org/cgi-shl/quotemeal.cgi?day=20110615, accessed March 12, 2021.

421 Adapted. https://www.christianity.com/church/church-history/timeline/1901-2000/jim-elliot-no-fool-11634862.html, accessed March 13, 2021.

422 https://www.brainyquote.com/quotes/jim_elliot_189244, accessed February 5, 2021.

423 Rogers, Ann. *Pittsburgh Post-Gazette,* "Ecuadoran Tribe Transformed After Killing of 5 Missionaries," January 08, 2006.

424 https://www.gracegems.org/Books2/dh08.htm, accessed April 4, 2020.

425 Begbie, Harold. *Life of William Booth: The Founder of the Salvation Army* (2 vols.). (London: MacMillan, 1920), 2:2.

426 Ibid.

427 D. C. Talk. *Jesus Freaks,* Revised and Updated ed. (Bethany House Publishers, October 27, 2020), 53–54. Adapted.

428 https://www.gracegems.org/Books2/dh08.htm, accessed April 4, 2020.

429 Francis Collier, William. *History of the British Empire (1870).* (Edinburg and New York: T. Nelson & Sons, 1876), 124.

430 Ibid.

431 Tan, P. L. *Encyclopedia of 7700 Illustrations: Signs of the Times.* (Garland, TX: Bible Communications, Inc., 1996), 787.

432 Ibid.

433 Ibid.

434 Mitchell, C. Ben. RM_Issue3_Apr2013_Mitchell.pdf, "Baptists, Conscience, and the Moral Marketplace," 64–65. https://www.uu.edu/journals/renewingminds/3/RM_Issue3_Apr2013_Mitchell.pdf, accessed February 25, 2021.

435 https://www.davidjeremiah.org/age-of-signs/wisdom-from-the-lions-den-10-quotes-from-persecuted-christians, accessed March 17, 2021.

436 Redpath, Alan. "The Price and Privilege of Discipleship," sermon delivered September 11, 1955, Moody Church, Chicago, Ill.

437 MacArthur, John. "Stephen: A Profile in Courage." gty.org, accessed February 13, 2021.

438 http://christian-quotes.ochristian.com/christian-quotes_ochristian.cgi?find=Christian-quotes-by-Charles+Spurgeon-on-Persecution, accessed February 13, 2021.

439 Piper, John. "Spreading Power Through Persecution," May 5, 1991. https://www.desiringgod.org/messages/spreading-power-through-persecution, accessed January 27, 2021.

440 Tertullian. *Apology 50,* c. A.D. 200.

441 https://suscopts.org/wiki/Types_of_Martyrs, accessed February 17, 2021.

442 Ironside, H. A. *Lectures on the Book of Revelation.* (Neptune, N. J.: Loizeaux Brothers, 1920), 41.

443 https://www.christianitytoday.com/history/people/martyrs/dietrich-bonhoeffer.html, accessed March 13, 2021.

444 Denison, Jim. *Denison Forum:* "What does the Bible Say about Politics?," October 1, 2020. https://www.denisonforum.org/resources/what-does-the-bible-say-about-politics/, accessed April 15, 2021.

445 https://www.christianquotes.info/quotes-by-topic/quotes-about-persecution/, accessed February 17, 2021.

[446] Criswell, W. A. "The Blood of Thy Martyr Stephen," Delivered July 10th, 1977. https://wacriswell.com/sermons/1977/the-blood-of-thy-martyr-stephen/, accessed February 17, 2021.

[447] Exell, J. S. *The Biblical Illustrator:* Luke. (Grand Rapids, MI: Baker Book House, 1952), 6:22–23.

[448] https://www.christianquotes.info/quotes-by-topic/quotes-about-persecution/, accessed February 17, 2021.

[449] https://www.kidsofcourage.com/?p=12900, accessed May 7, 2021.

[450] https://www.christianquotes.info/quotes-by-topic/quotes-about-persecution/, accessed February 17, 2021.

[451] Keller, Timothy. *The Reason For God.* (New York, NY: Dutton, 2008), 234.

[452] Henry, Matthew. *Complete Commentary on the Whole Bible,* 1706, Matthew 17:20.

[453] *Notes on the Bible* by Albert Barnes [1834], Matthew 17:20.

[454] Spence-Jones, H. D. M. (Ed.). *Philippians.* (London; New York: Funk & Wagnalls Company, 1909), 20.

[455] *Notes on the Bible* by Albert Barnes [1834], Daniel 3:16.

[456] Spurgeon, C. H. "God's People in the Furnace" (Sermon delivered August 12, 1885). *New Park Street Pulpit,* Volume 1.

[457] Henry, M. *Matthew Henry's Commentary on the Whole Bible: Complete and Unabridged in One Volume.* (Peabody: Hendrickson, 1994), 1630.

[458] https://www.christianquotes.info/quotes-by-topic/quotes-about-satan/, accessed March 19, 2021.

[459] Morgan, R. J. *Nelson's Annual Preacher's Sourcebook,* 2003 Edition. (Nashville: Thomas Nelson Publishers, 2002), 400.

[460] Spurgeon, C. H. "The Reward of the Righteous" (Sermon), delivered January 21, 1866. https://www.spurgeon.org/resource-library/sermons/the-reward-of-the-righteous/#flipbook/, accessed April 02, 2021.

[461] Criswell, W. A. "The Martyr's Seal" (Revelation 6:9–11), delivered April 1, 1962. https://wacriswell.com/sermons/1962/the-martyr-s-seal1/, accessed February 17, 2021.

[462] https://quotefancy.com/quote/1103774, accessed May 7, 2021.

[463] Rogers, Adrian. "Preparing for the Coming Persecution." https://www.oneplace.com/ministries/love-worth-finding/read/articles/preparing-for-the-coming-persecution-17488.html, accessed February 9, 2021.

[464] https://quotefancy.com/quote/1650505, accessed May 7, 2021.

[465] *Notes on the Bible* by Albert Barnes [1834], Revelation 2:10.

466 Criswell, W. A. "The Martyred Christians of Smyrna" (Delivered July 23rd, 1961). https://wacriswell.com/sermons/1961/the-martyred-christians-of-smyrna/, accessed February 13, 2021.

467 *Notes on the Bible* by Albert Barnes [1834], Revelation 2:10.

468 Criswell, W. A. "The Martyred Christians of Smyrna" (Delivered July 23rd, 1961). https://wacriswell.com/sermons/1961/the-martyred-christians-of-smyrna/, accessed February 13, 2021.

469 Ironside, H. A. *Lectures on the Book of Revelation.* (Neptune, N. J.: Loizeaux Brothers, 1920), 41–42.

470 *Notes on the Bible* by Albert Barnes [1834], Revelation 2:10.

471 Clarke, Adam. *Commentary on the Bible.* (1831), Revelation 2:10.

472 Exell, J. S. *The Biblical Illustrator: Revelation.* (Grand Rapids, MI: Baker Book House, 1952), 2:10.

473 Ibid.

474 D. C. Talk. *Jesus Freaks,* Revised and Updated ed. (Bethany House Publishers, October 27, 2020), 53–54. Adapted.

475 Spurgeon, C. H. "God's People in the Furnace" (Sermon delivered August 12, 1885). *New Park Street Pulpit,* Volume 1.

CPSIA information can be obtained
at www.ICGtesting.com
Printed in the USA
BVHW032225040222
628152BV00005B/96